The Law
and You

The Law and You

*A Commentary on the
Ten Commandments*

by

Reimar A.C. Schultze

CTO Books
PO Box 825
Kokomo, Indiana 46903 USA

All Scripture quotations are taken from the King James Bible.

Front cover: Rose Image Copyright ID 64363861 inxti, 2013
p. 30: Rose Image Copyright ID 64363861 inxti, 2013
p. 44: Idol Image - Public Domain
p. 54: Sea Beach Image Copyright ID 109929869 Yuriy Kulik, 2013
p. 68: Church Image Copyright ID 12091567 Russell Shively, 2013
p. 84: Happy Family Copyright ID 137945813 turkishblue, 2013
p. 100: Dagger Image Copyright ID 74452030 Senol Yamen, 2013
p. 112: Rings Image Copyright ID 103420760 tristan3D, 2013
p. 134: Bitten Red Apple Image Copyright ID 105445550 valzan, 2013
p. 146: Candle Image Copyright ID 78566707 Mihalec, 2013
p. 160: Angel Image Copyright 103686620 Babin, 2013
Used under license from Shutterstock.com

The Law and You: A Commentary on the Ten Commandments
Copyright © 2013 Reimar A. C. Schultze
All Rights Reserved.
ISBN-13: 978-0-9724411-5-5
E-PDF ISBN-13: 978-0-9724411-6-2
E-PUB ISBN-13: 978-0-9724411-7-9
LCCN: 2013942728

Published by:
CTO Books
PO Box 825
Kokomo, Indiana 46903 USA
www.ctobooks.com

Publisher's Cataloging-in-Publication
(Provided by Quality Books, Inc.)

Schultze, Reimar A. C.
   The law and you : a commentary on the Ten commandments / by Reimar A.C. Schultze.
   p. cm.
   LCCN 2013942728
   ISBN 978-0-972-4411-5-5

   1. Ten commandments--Commentaries.   I. Title.

BS1285.53.S38 2013   222'.1607
                             QBI13-600096

Printed in the United States of America.

Contents

Foreword..vii

Preface...ix

The Ten Commandments................................xiii

Origin and Purpose of Law...............................17

First Commandment..31

Second Commandment......................................45

Third Commandment...55

Fourth Commandment.......................................69

Fifth Commandment..85

Sixth Commandment..101

Seventh Commandment...................................113

Eighth Commandment.....................................135

Ninth Commandment.......................................147

Tenth Commandment......................................161

Conclusion... 172

Additional Resources......................................176

Foreword

At one of the greatest events in the history of mankind, God spoke to a man named Moses, and gave him the Ten Commandments as a set of guidelines for how to live life. They are simple, exact, and accurate words that lead us on the pathway to intimacy with God, and fulfillment in all our relationships. These life-giving words changed the world because they came from the heart and mouth of our Heavenly Father. Being once spoken in power, they will never return to Him void.

In this book, Pastor Schultze endeavors to expound and capture the true meaning of the Ten Words, first given to the offspring of Abraham who were in search of a homeland. Though some may consider them outdated enlightenment spoken to a Jewish leader long ago, these Words have echoed from Mount Sinai down through the halls of history and have called all of us to the altar of God. I, along with Pastor Schultze, believe they still hold truth, faith, and life for all peoples of all time. And I appreciate him taking on the difficult challenge of bringing fresh insights on these Words to us today.

And these insights – given by the Holy Spirit to Pastor Schultze – have filtered through his spiritual journey as he has spent much time in prayer and waiting before God's throne. This book is not likely to "tickle your ears," but its direct, uncompromising approach will speak to your heart, and change your life for eternity. Read and meditate upon these words – you will not be disappointed by what you find.

Pastor J. Mark Donnelly, D.Min., Ret. Ch., LtCol., USAF, Teaching Pastor of Shema Christ Fellowship, Head of Pastoral Ministries at South Florida Bible College and Theological Seminary.

Preface

Seldom in recent times have we seen lawlessness eat its way into the moral fiber of our churches, as today. Perhaps this is the reason why the Lord has laid it upon my heart to write on the Ten Commandments. Each time before my pen would touch the paper, I would give myself to a few moments of audible praise to get the clutter of the world out of my mind. I wanted to hear from God because it is only by the Holy Spirit that we can be fed. Along with this, I am thankful for the many people who have prayed me through towards the completion of this work.

Particularly challenging to me was the Seventh Commandment on adultery, because the question whether a divorced person has a biblical right to remarry has not been satisfactorily answered for many. The Fourth Commandment on honoring your father and mother has also received extraordinary attention because we live in a world where there is an epidemic of broken homes. Then there is the Sabbath. Do we still need it? Does God still want us to have it?

Throughout this book, I brought in the words of Jesus on these laws, how He masterfully unfolded them for all of us as no one else could.

The rose on the front cover is to remind the reader that law can never be properly understood outside the context of love.

The size of the book was intentionally designed to be small, to be easily transportable on the mission fields of the world. The questions at the end of each chapter are given to encourage Bible studies and group discussions.

As you begin to read this book, I want you to take notice that the most far-reaching, earthshaking events in all of human history were the giving of the Law at Mount Sinai and the fulfilling of the Law at Mount Calvary.

At the giving of the Law, the Bible says:

"And all the people saw the thunderings, and the lightnings, and the noise of the trumpet, and the mountain smoking: and when the people saw it, they removed, and stood afar off" (Exodus 20:18).

At the fulfilling of the Law, the Bible says:

"Jesus, when he had cried again with a loud voice, yielded up the ghost. And, behold, the veil of the temple was rent in twain from the top to the bottom; and the earth did quake, and the rocks rent; And the graves were opened; and many bodies of the saints which slept arose, And came out of the graves after his

resurrection, and went into the holy city, and appeared unto many" (Matthew 27:50-53).

Because of these very powerful divine manifestations surrounding the giving and fulfilling of the Law, every man should be compelled to explore and search out the Law's personal and priceless significance to his own life.

It is through law that we know that we live in a moral universe, that we begin to know God, that our relationship to Him is defined and that we are taught how to live justly, holy and humbly before our God.

Reimar A.C. Schultze

The Ten Commandments

1. Thou shalt have no other gods before me.

2. Thou shalt not make unto thee any graven image.

3. Thou shalt not take the name of the LORD thy God in vain.

4. Remember the Sabbath Day, to keep it holy.

5. Honour thy Father and thy Mother.

6. Thou shalt not Kill.

7. Thou shalt not Commit Adultery.

8. Thou shalt not Steal.

9. Thou shalt not Bear False Witness against thy neighbour.

10. Thou shalt not Covet.

The Law
and You

Origin and Purpose of Law

No law in the world can match the wisdom, beauty, strength and goodwill of the Ten Commandments. Any family or nation which gives these laws their due respect is certain to invite the blessing and friendship of God Almighty.

Before we approach the subject of law, we must make a distinction between three types of laws:

1. Natural laws,
2. Spiritual laws,
3. Human laws.

1. Natural laws pertain to our physical universe: to that which we see, hear, handle, weigh and measure. We find these laws operating in physics, chemistry, biology and so on. Everything God created, the whole physical universe and man, are bound by these laws. Only God can override them, and when He does, we call that a miracle. Natural laws will come to an end with the eventual destruction of this universe (2 Peter 3:10).

2. Spiritual laws relate to the God/man relationship, to man's relationship with his fellows, and to the operation of the kingdom of God. At the heart of spiritual laws are moral laws which are

the primary focus of this book. Moral laws pertain to right and wrong. The Ten Commandments are moral law.

3. <u>Human laws</u> are man-made. They are the product of civil courts, industry, labor unions and such like.

The Necessity of Law

Lawlessness leads to chaos. Without natural laws the physical universe cannot operate. Similarly, the spiritual universe is governed by laws. Since God is the center of the universe, and since He is holy, He has set boundaries by which He cannot tolerate anything which defiles, corrupts or distorts that holiness. On the day He created man, God also established moral law – limits for man's behavior. That means that before Adam saw his first golden sunset on his first day, he found himself in a God/man relationship governed by law:

"And the LORD God commanded the man, saying, Of every tree of the garden thou mayest freely eat: But of the tree of the knowledge of good and evil, thou shalt not eat of it: for in the day that thou eatest thereof thou shalt surely die" (Genesis 2:16-17).

From this event forward it is evident that every man is born into a moral universe where

ORIGIN AND PURPOSE OF LAW

obedience to law will keep him in fellowship with God and disobedience will cause him to lose that fellowship. This helps us to know that at the very heart of law is a call to obedience. The measure of our love to God is in our obedience to what He asks us to do. From Genesis on, we learn that the entire spectrum of blessings and curses hinges on one solitary condition: obedience! This is proclaimed over and over in the Bible:

"And it shall come to pass, if thou shalt hearken diligently unto the voice of the LORD thy God, to observe and to do all his commandments which I command thee this day, that the LORD thy God will set thee on high above all nations of the earth: And all these blessings shall come on thee, and overtake thee, if thou shalt hearken unto the voice of the LORD thy God" (Deuteronomy 28:1-2).

"But it shall come to pass, if thou wilt not hearken unto the voice of the LORD thy God, to observe to do all his commandments and his statutes which I command thee this day; that all these curses shall come upon thee, and overtake thee" (Deuteronomy 28:15).

"If ye love me, keep my commandments" (John 14:15).

"Know ye not, that to whom ye yield yourselves servants to obey, his servants ye are to whom ye obey; whether of sin unto death, or of obedience unto righteousness?" (Romans 6:16).

Therefore, the "origin" of law is not to be found in some antiquated courthouse in some town somewhere in ancient time, but in Paradise itself before man ever raised his head against God Almighty. The "why" of law comes out of God's holiness. The ultimate "purpose" of law is to keep man in the garden of God's fellowship, holiness and love forever (Deuteronomy 5:29, 33).

Consequences of Disobedience

Although our first parents continued to worship and believe in God after they were expelled from the Garden of Eden, they became the ancestors of all those who believe without obeying. This is devilish faith because the devil also believes, but he will not obey. Faith without the works of obedience began in the Garden. This false faith has taken millions into eternal darkness.

Adam's and Eve's disobedience to law precipitated the greatest fall of man conceivable to the human mind. When this couple ate of the forbidden fruit, evil entered into the spiritual bloodstream of humanity in such immensity, qualitatively and quantitatively, that it actually resulted in the first-born human child becoming a murderer. Since that fall, here are some of the things that are found in every man: selfishness, covetousness, dishonesty, greed, anger, hatred, pride, fornication, strife, envy, jealousy, adultery, idolatry, witchcraft, drunkenness, rebellion, murder, and such like. There in the Garden, in the twinkling of an eye, one disobedience brought man from being in the likeness of God, from the highest state of purity, to the deepest level of depravity. This indictment has thus been forever on the human race:

"The heart is deceitful above all things, and desperately wicked: who can know it?" (Jeremiah 17:9).

It is this explosion of the wickedness of man that caused God to bring a devastating flood upon the whole earth:

"And God saw that the wickedness of man was great in the earth, and that every imagination of the thoughts of his heart was only evil continually. And it repented the LORD that he had made man on the earth, and it grieved him at his heart. And the LORD said, I will destroy man whom I have created from the face of the

earth; both man, and beast, and the creeping thing, and the fowls of the air; for it repenteth me that I have made them" (Genesis 6:5-7).

Only righteous Noah and his family were spared from this flood. Can you hear the desperate cry from the heart of God for obedience:

"O that there were such an heart in them, that they would fear me, and keep all my commandments always, that it might be well with them, and with their children for ever!" (Deuteronomy 5:29).

The Journey Toward the Ten Commandments

Although disobedience to law took man to a precipice of total annihilation, God did not give up on man. God had a plan for the ages that would offer man salvation from his inner perversion to bring him back into the garden of His presence, to become His eternal bride.

About 400 years after Noah, when man had multiplied again on the face of the earth, God sought out another man whom He could trust. He found one in a sheep farmer named Abraham in the land of the Chaldeans. Abraham was a solitary beacon of light and truth in a world wholly steeped in idolatry again. It was because Abraham loved God and his ear was open to His voice, that God

ORIGIN AND PURPOSE OF LAW

was able to continue His divine plans through him. God made a covenant (a contract) with Abraham, that through his offspring all the families of the earth would be blessed (Genesis 12:3).

In another 430 years, Abraham's descendants (the Hebrews) had multiplied exceedingly to become a nation people now living as slaves in Egypt. Among them was the next key man through whom God could further His purposes: Moses. It was Moses who led the Hebrews out of Egyptian slavery to gather them together in an open desert at the foot of one of the bare, ragged mountains at Sinai. It is here that God for the first time addressed His covenant people as a nation. In His inaugural address, He claimed His Lordship over them and gave them the Ten Commandments which became their constitution and code of law.

Having considered the origin and purpose of law, the cost of disobedience and the journey from Paradise to Mount Sinai, let us now observe the uniqueness by which these Ten Commandments were delivered from God to man. There is nothing like this in the world. By observing this process, we learn much about God: about His love, His condescension, His attention to details and His earnestness in seeking to draw us into His very heart. Understanding God helps us to understand

His laws. Look at the difference by which these laws were given, compared to how any other sets of laws were delivered from law givers to their people.

The Unique Way the Ten Commandments Were Given

1. The Ten Commandments are uniquely different than any other laws known by man, because they were given to us by God. And because these commandments had their origin with God, they were written with eternity in mind.

2. These Ten Commandments are uniquely different from all the other laws of the world in the way they were written. In fact, these are the only documents in the world not written by man, nor with an instrument of writing. Rather, they were written with fire by the finger of God on two tablets of stone as a covenant agreement or contract between God and man. That speaks of the permanence of the God/man relationship. To violate these commandments will always be wrong. It will always be wrong to commit idolatry, to steal, to bear false witness, to kill, to covet, etc. This is why we also find all of the Ten Commandments in the New Testament as well. The Jews had 613 other laws called the Laws of Moses. But they were written by man on parchment, indicating their temporary nature. They were for the most part to

serve Israel only until the great Law Giver would send His Son Jesus into the world. But these commandments on stone were personally handed from the hands of God to the hands of Moses. They were written in the first person (you) so as to highlight that through them God is speaking to all of us individually.

3. The Ten Commandments are different than any other laws, including the Laws of Moses, in <u>the way by which they were placed amongst the people</u> of Israel. The book of Exodus tells us that God ordered the construction of a special box to hold the tablets of stone. This box was to be called the Ark of the Covenant because these two tablets represent a covenant agreement between God the greater and man the lesser, not to be broken but by the penalty of death. This box was 3 3/4 feet long, 2 1/4 feet wide and 2 1/4 feet high. It was made of chittum wood and it was to be covered by a slab of gold, called the mercy seat. <u>This is the only box God has ever designed</u>. It was through the sprinkling of the blood on the mercy seat that repentant man could find a new beginning.

4. The Ten Commandments were unique in that the box that contained them became <u>a meeting place of God with man</u>. God said to Moses and His people:

"And there I will meet with thee..." (Exodus 25:22).

Here men could have fellowship with the Almighty, in the presence of the God of law and mercy. For man can never come into the presence of God outside of a moral context. It is here where man's disobedience is dealt with and it is here where forgiveness becomes possible.

5. The Ten Commandments are different than others because it is <u>by them that all other laws will be judged</u>. They were given as the foundation for every legal system in the world and for the benefit of all mankind. Where they are honored, nations prosper; where they are violated, nations suffer.

6. The Ten Commandments distinguish themselves from all others in that <u>they are perfectly applicable for every generation</u>: to every cultural and tribal group in every successive civilization. They are universally binding on every man on the face of the earth. God has even written them into the heart of every man at birth (Romans 2:15).

Law and Love

The perception that the Old Testament is about "law" and the New Testament is about "love" is most erroneous. This perception is proven incorrect when we consider that at the same time that God called men to obey His Ten Laws, He also commanded them to love Him with all their hearts. This is the reason why Moses in his farewell address to Israel cited law and love in tandem. In Deuteronomy 5, he quotes the Ten Commandments, in Deuteronomy 6, we see him quoting the premier laws of love:

"Hear, O Israel: The LORD our God is one LORD: And thou shalt love the LORD thy God with all thine heart, and with all thy soul, and with all thy might. And these words, which I command thee this day, shall be in thine heart. And thou shalt teach them diligently unto thy children, and shalt talk of them when thou sittest in thine house, and when thou walkest by the way, and when thou liest down, and when thou risest up" (Deuteronomy 6:4-7).

We cannot be united with God except by law and love. Yet, of the two, the law of love is more demanding than all other laws in the world put together. How love and law are linked together is also illustrated by the words of Jesus. He reaffirms the law/love connection of Deuteronomy for this church age:

"He that hath my commandments, and keepeth them, he it is that loveth me: and he that loveth

me shall be loved of my Father, and I will love him, and will manifest myself to him" (John 14:21).

Notice three vital points that emerge from this scripture:

- The keeping of His commandments are proof of our love to Him.
- Our love to Him will be rewarded by His love and His Father's love to us.
- The outcome of our loving obedience to Jesus will be His making residence in us.

In other words, new life in Christ cannot be obtained nor maintained without a serious commitment to obedience. Obedience is essential for fellowship with God. God gives every human born into the world both the grace and power to obey.

Because of this, Cain was just as able to obey God as Abel. The problem is not that man cannot obey God, but that he does not want to. If man were not able to obey God, God could not call him guilty. Even before the Holy Spirit was given, Jesus said to His Father that His disciples had obeyed Him in everything and that He was happy with them:

"...they have kept thy word. ...and I am glorified in them" (John 17:6, 10).

ORIGIN AND PURPOSE OF LAW

Obedience is not the result of our salvation or Spirit baptism, it is the prerequisite for both!

*"And we are his witnesses of these things; and so is also the Holy Ghost, whom God hath given **to them that obey him**"* (Acts 5:32 [emphasis added]).

Once we have obeyed and received the Holy Spirit, then Christlikeness will be the fruit of our lives.

Paul said, *"...love is the fulfilling of the law"* (Romans 13:10). Law without love kills. It killed Jesus. It kills everything that is of the Spirit. On the other hand, love without law is permissive and unholy. It also kills everything that is of God. In the eyes of God, love and law are the best of friends living happily in the same house together. They need to live happily together in your heart as well.

Finally, it is worth noting that what we call the Ten Commandments, the Jews call the Ten Words. Therefore we use these expressions interchangeably.

Now, having said all this, let us spell out what specifically God had in mind when He put His laws into the most extravagant jewelry box ever given to man.

God and God Alone

*"No man can serve two masters:
for either he will hate the one, and love the other;
or else he will hold to the one,
and despise the other."*

—Matthew 6:24

First Commandment

"I am the LORD thy God,

which have brought thee out of the land of Egypt, out of the house of bondage.

Thou shalt have no other gods before me."

—Exodus 20:2-3

This means that you shall not have any other gods beside, before or instead of the God who brought Israel out of Egypt. It means the God of Israel is the only true God:

"I am the LORD, and there is none else, there is no God beside me..." (Isaiah 45:5).

This First Commandment does away with polytheism. It annuls all other gods which men worship, declaring them to be nothing other than a figment of man's imagination:

"They are vanity, and the work of errors: in the time of their visitation they shall perish" (Jeremiah 10:15).

What Gives God the Right to Say, "I Am the Only One, and You Need No Other gods?"

Here are two good reasons:

1. <u>The God of Israel is the creator and sustainer of all things</u>; all energy and life proceed from Him:

"He hath made the earth by his power, he hath established the world by his wisdom, and hath stretched out the heavens by his discretion" (Jeremiah 10:12).

"For by him were all things created, that are in heaven, and that are in earth, visible and invisible, whether they be thrones, or dominions, or principalities, or powers: all things were created by him, and for him: And he is before all things, and by him all things consist" (Colossians 1:16-17).

If God were to cease His existence, the whole universe would fly apart. All life is from God. Simply stated, we are because God is.

Because all things came out of Him, and because we were created and sustained by Him and for Him, our hearts should unceasingly do obeisance before Him. As the ancient Ark of the Covenant became the central point around which Israel camped, so must God be the center of all we seek, say and do. Since we are His offspring, we need to dwell in Him, and He, in turn, takes pleasure by dwelling in us. We in Him and He in us is the essence of Christianity (John 15:4; 1 John 4:13-16).

We find no rest until we find rest in Him. We are homeless until we find our home in Him. A man without God is like a ship without a rudder, a farmer without land and a fish without water.

2. God has credentials! Anybody who claims to be somebody needs credentials to prove their claim is true. When God gave the Ten Commandments, He reminded His people of the credentials He displayed when He brought them out of slavery in Egypt. He delivered them from Pharaoh through ten impressive miracles (Exodus 7-12). Then He opened the sea for them to walk through on dry ground. Credentials! Then He went with them into the wilderness and fed them with bread from the sky and gave them water out of a rock. He led them during the day with a cloud and at night with a pillar of fire. Credentials! His credentials show through His actions.

At Mount Sinai, God introduced His

commandments to them by reminding them that He is not a bondage-maker but a bondage-breaker:

"I am the LORD thy God, which have brought thee out of the land of Egypt, out of the house of bondage" (Exodus 20:2).

Is it any wonder, then, that the Jews make this scripture their First Commandment?[1] The Jews embraced these commandments as a roadway to freedom, delivering them from their enemies and from their own ways by their undivided allegiance to God. They received these laws as a gift of love. They received these laws as a bride receives the most exquisite bouquet of roses from her lover. From the day of the birth of the Jewish nation, these laws have been delightful to their hearts and food for their meditations. May it be so for us:

"Thy statutes have been my songs in the house of my pilgrimage" (Psalm 119:54).

"Unless thy law had been my delights, I should then have perished in mine affliction" (Psalm 119:92).

"O how love I thy law! it is my meditation all the day" (Psalm 119:97).

The Apostle Paul, a devout Jew and a chief Apostle of Christ, puts it this way:

FIRST COMMANDMENT

"Wherefore the law is holy, and the commandment holy, and just, and good" (Romans 7:12).

Having hundreds of years of biblical history behind us, let us now look at specific instances of God's interactions with man to confirm His magnificent and benevolent nature toward His people. God wants to be with us in the same manner He was with Israel. Here is the kind of God Israel had:

- Israel had a God who communicated with His people (Genesis 12:1).
- Israel had a God who taught them (Isaiah 54:13).
- Israel had a God who made a way for them to pass through the Red Sea (Exodus 14:21-22) and the Jordan River (Joshua 3:14-17) on dry ground.
- Israel had a God who sheltered them from the sun (Exodus 13:21), provided bread from the sky (Exodus 16:4) and provided water from a rock (Exodus 17:3-7).
- Israel had a God who made bitter waters sweet (Exodus 15:22-25).

- Israel had a God who made the sun and moon stand still (Joshua 10:12-13).

- Israel had a God who cured lepers (Numbers 12:11-15) and healed them from serpents' bites (Numbers 21:4-9).

- Israel had a God who made a man walk 40 days and 40 nights on one meal (1 Kings 19:8).

- Israel had a God who multiplied a widow's oil to deliver her from her creditors (2 Kings 4:7).

- Israel had a God who noticed the tears of a distraught woman and spared her from losing her son (Genesis 21:16-19).

- Israel had a God who preserved them in the fiery furnaces (Daniel 3:19-27) and the lions dens of life (Daniel 6:16-23).

- Israel has a God who can heal a broken heart (Isaiah 61:1).

- Israel has a God who can forgive sins and remove them as far as the east is from the west (Psalm 103:12).

- Israel's God promised to give them a new heart and put a right spirit within them (Ezekiel 36:26).

God has credentials!

This Is the God Israel Experienced; This Is Also Our God.

God said to us all:

"For I am the LORD, I change not..." (Malachi 3:6).

Biblical scholars have described the attributes of God by saying "God is" as follows:

Sovereign, All-sufficient, Immense, Infinite, All-knowing, All-powerful, Perfect, Immutable, Incomprehensible, Transcendent, Impartial, All-pervasive, Loving, Merciful, Long-suffering, Gracious, Holy, Righteous, Just, and an Avenger of the wicked.

All of these attributes are everlasting and all of them are essential. Truly there is none like our God:

"For who in the heaven can be compared unto the LORD? who among the sons of the mighty can be likened unto the LORD?" (Psalm 89:6).

"Bless the LORD, O my soul. O LORD my God, thou art very great; thou art clothed with honour and majesty. Who coverest thyself with light as with a garment: who stretchest out the heavens like a curtain: Who layeth the beams of his chambers in the waters: who maketh

the clouds his chariot: who walketh upon the wings of the wind" (Psalm 104:1-3).

What other god can boast such credentials? What other god can compare to the God of Israel in benevolence and condescension to the children of man? And this indeed is the God who ultimately offered His own Son on a cross to invite us to fellowship with Him in the courts of heaven forever:

"Thou shalt have no other gods before me."

How Do We Recognize that Something Has Become a god to Us?

If there is any one thing in our life that takes precedence over our loving, listening to and following Jesus, we are in idolatry. Every time Israel left her God, she always returned to idolatry. Every generation and culture has their gods. We live in a dangerous world of idolatry. Nearly everyone Jesus met was an idolater. Let us look at what forms of idolatry Jesus encountered during His earthly visitation.

MONEY was a god to the rich young ruler who came to Jesus to be saved. When Jesus asked him to give it up, the young man refused (Matthew 19:22). The Apostle Paul also told Timothy:

"For the love of money is the root of all evil..."
(1 Timothy 6:10).

Jesus asked some people to follow Him, but their PLANS were their gods. One wanted to bury his father first (Matthew 8:21-22). Another wanted time to bid his family farewell. Yet another used his wedding as an excuse for not following Jesus when called (Luke 14:20).

To some Pharisees and Scribes, TRADITION was their god. Jesus said that while following their traditions, they neglected the commandments of God (Mark 7:5-9).

To others, FAMILY was a god. Jesus told a large crowd that unless they would love Him more than family, they could not be His disciples (Luke 14:26). Shortly after this, Jesus gave a new definition of family by saying:

"For whosoever shall do the will of my Father which is in heaven, the same is my brother, and sister, and mother" (Matthew 12:50).

We cease to be God's children if we allow family pressures, traditions and plans to interfere with what God has willed and purposed for us.

To some, FINANCIAL SECURITY was their god (Luke 12:16-22). Our security is to be in seeking first the kingdom of God and His righteousness; and all necessary things shall be added unto us (Matthew 6:33).

RELIGIOUS COMMITMENTS can become a god to us, causing us to neglect the needy about us (Luke 10:30-33).

To many people of high social status and education, PLEASING MAN is their god (John 12:42-43). The elders of Jerusalem were addicted to "political correctness." They feared losing the favor of man. They did not join themselves to Jesus for fear of losing their social status. Doing so would have caused them to be put out of the synagogue (John 9:22).

These were some of the gods with which Jesus had to contend. He lived in a world of idolatry. Now, let us name some gods more prevalent in our days.

PLEASURES or INTERESTS are a god to many people; to some it is sports, to others it is fishing, golfing, gardening or auto racing. To others, pets, television programs, movies or the Internet are gods. Yet to others, it is excelling in grades, education, social position, stylish dress, or a job. Whatever awakens our greatest interest and is more important to us than God, is a god to us. Whatever takes us from prayer or worship is a god to us.

Here Are Three Checks that Reveal if We Have Another god in Our Lives.

We must look at our <u>bank account</u>, at the use of our <u>time</u>, at the energy, direction and intensity of our <u>passions</u>. John the Apostle also groups all gods into just three categories:

"...the lust of the flesh, and the lust of the eyes, and the pride of life, in not of the Father, but is of the world" (1 John 2:16).

If we have other gods, we violate the law of love. If we do not love God with all our heart, soul, mind and strength, we fall short of being Christians. We are pretenders and hypocrites. In the Old Testament, the penalty for idolatry was death by stoning. In the New Testament, it is exclusion from the kingdom of God. In both cases, it means banishment to an eternal hell. God will not tolerate rivals or competing loves. <u>Jesus must always be our first love</u>:

"No man can serve two masters: for either he will hate the one, and love the other; or else he will hold to the one, and despise the other. Ye cannot serve God and mammon [riches]" (Matthew 6:24 [emphasis added]).

"But the fearful, and unbelieving, and the abominable, and murderers, and whoremongers [sexually immoral], and sorcerers, and IDOLATERS, and all liars, shall

have their part in the lake which burneth with fire and brimstone: which is the second death" (Revelation 21:8 [emphasis added]).

"Thou shalt have no other gods before me."

The devil tempts every single person to worship something other than God Himself. The devil took Jesus to a high mountain early in His ministry, pointed to all the kingdoms of the world, and said to Him:

"If thou therefore wilt worship me, all shall be thine" (Luke 4:7).

The devil promised to give everything to Jesus to stop Him from worshipping His Father, and he will also do so to you. Beware!

"Having no other gods before me" is a heavenly commandment that precedes all of the other commandments. If we keep this one directive, we will be well on our way to keeping all the others. If we do not start here, there is no other place for us to start.

<u>Either we are all for God, or we are not for God at all</u>.

Footnotes:
1 Numbers for the commandments were not affixed to them by God, but by man. Jews, Catholics and Protestants attached different numbers to them.

Questions to Ponder:

1. What gives the Lord the right to declare that He is the only God?

2. How do we recognize if there are other gods in our lives?

3. In what sense is this commandment life to us?

God Is a Spirit

"God is a Spirit: and they that worship him must worship him in spirit and in truth.

John 4:24

Second Commandment

"I am the LORD thy God...

Thou shalt not make unto thee any graven image,

or any likeness of anything that is in heaven above, or that is in the earth beneath, or that is in the water under the earth: Thou shalt not bow down thyself to them, nor serve them: for I the LORD thy God am a jealous God, visiting the iniquity of the fathers upon the children unto the third and fourth generation of them that hate me; And shewing mercy unto thousands of them that love me, and keep my commandments."

—Exodus 20:4-6

The First Commandment prohibits us from HAVING any other gods; this Second Commandment prohibits us from MAKING other gods. This commandment exclusively deals with image-making and it contains three important points:

1. The making of images;

2. The worship of images;

3. The penalty for making and worshipping images.

"Thou shalt not make unto thee any graven image."

A "graven" image is a carved image, an idol. It is something that represents a god but is not. It can be in the form of a human, an animal, a plant or any object. At the giving of the Ten Commandments, Israel's neighbors only knew image worship. For the Canaanites, the image was Baal; for the Philistines, it was Dagon; for the Babylonians, it was Enlil and Marduk; and for the Egyptians, the images were Osiris and Isis. Most of these cultures had many gods and goddesses. The concept of "no images" was revolutionary in the days of Moses.

In A.D. 70, when the Roman General Titus (who later became Caesar) captured Jerusalem and stormed into the temple, the Romans were expecting to find the statue of the God of Israel.

SECOND COMMANDMENT

They were stunned and amazed to find that there was no image of God in the temple! The God of Israel cannot be represented by an image. Mortal man cannot see Him. Moses reminded his people of how God visited them before giving them the Ten Commandments:

"Take ye therefore good heed unto yourselves; for ye <u>saw no manner of similitude</u> [no likeness of God]*on the day that the LORD spake unto you in Horeb out of the midst of the fire: Lest ye corrupt yourselves, and make you a graven image, the similitude of any figure, the likeness of male or female"* (Deuteronomy 4:15-16 [emphasis added]).

Jesus reaffirmed that God is invisible to human eyes when He told a Samaritan woman:

"God is a Spirit: and they that worship him must worship him in spirit and in truth" (John 4:24).

Man must be born again in order to worship God in the spirit (John 3:3-7), and he must also be subject to the character and will of God to worship Him in truth (Psalm 24:3-4).

There is nothing in all of creation that reveals God's face to us. Even if we take everything God has created in the heavens, the earth and the sea, we will never be able to assemble a picture of the face of God. However, we understand many of His fundamental attributes from His resplendent creation. Nature gives evidence of His intelligence, wisdom, power, benevolence and extravagance:

"The heavens declare the glory of God; and the firmament sheweth his handywork" (Psalm 19:1).

Because the heavens and the firmament are created things, God has forbidden the worship of them. He wants us to worship Him, the Creator. If you have an image of a god in your home, even if it is just for decoration, destroy it.

Jacob had two wives. Leah was God's choice for him, but Jacob chose Rachel, an image worshipper. She brought idolatry into Jacob's family, preventing them from receiving all God had for them. Image worship grieves the Holy Spirit. It always defiles. Again and again, God demanded the destruction of images:

"But ye shall destroy their altars, break their images, and cut down their groves" (Exodus 34:13).

"The graven images of their gods shall ye burn with fire: thou shalt not desire the silver or gold that is on them, nor take it unto thee, lest thou

be snared therein: for it is an abomination to the LORD thy God" (Deuteronomy 7:25).

"Thou shalt not bow down thyself to them, nor serve them."

Again, God calls for an end of religious worship as it had been known throughout the nations. The Apostle Paul warns that in the worship of nature, the glory of God is assigned to something that is mere creation. This leads to corruption of the mind, darkness in the heart and the perversion of truth. In his letter to the Romans, Paul states that no one is born an atheist: he knows that there is a God by nature's testimony and because His laws are written into every man's heart (Psalm 19:1-4; John 1:9; Romans 2:15). Unbelief in God begins with man's failure to acknowledge and praise Him from the beginning:

"Because that, when they knew God, they glorified him not as God, neither were thankful; but became vain in their imaginations, and their foolish heart was darkened" (Romans 1:21).

"And changed the glory of the uncorruptible God into an image made like to corruptible man, and to birds, and fourfooted beasts, and creeping things" (Romans 1:23).

Again, image worship defiles the heart and soul of man. The end result of such perversion is total moral corruption, God giving these transgressors over to their just reward:

"And even as they did not like to retain God in their knowledge, <u>God gave them over to a reprobate</u> [depraved] <u>mind</u>, to do those things which are not convenient [fitting];

Being filled with all unrighteousness, fornication, wickedness, covetousness, maliciousness; full of envy, murder, debate, deceit, malignity [evil-mindedness]; *whisperers,*

Backbiters, haters of God, despiteful, proud, boasters, inventors of evil things, disobedient to parents,

Without understanding, covenant breakers, without natural affection, implacable [unforgiving], *unmerciful:*

Who knowing the judgment of God, that they which commit such things are worthy of death, not only do the same, but have pleasure in them that do them" (Romans 1:28-32 [emphasis added]).

God is incorruptible! To create a corruptible image of God is an enormous misrepresentation of Him. When you worship an image, you do not worship God.

God taunts these image makers and worshippers by saying:

"The idols of the heathen are silver and gold, the work of men's hands.

They have mouths, but they speak not; eyes have they, but they see not;

They have ears, but they hear not; neither is there any breath in their mouths.

They that make them are like unto them: so is every one that trusteth in them" (Psalm 135:15-18).

The Penalty for Making and Worshipping an Image:

"...for I the LORD thy God am a jealous God, visiting the iniquity of the fathers upon the children unto the third and fourth generation of them that hate me" (Exodus 20:5).

Image worship brings a generational curse with it. If any man worships an image, a curse comes upon him which will be passed on to his children and children's children, even to the fourth generation. However, God provides an escape from this generational curse in the last verse of this commandment by offering mercy to those who repent:

"And shewing mercy unto thousands of them that love me, and keep my commandments" (Exodus 20:6).

Going back to Genesis, it is interesting to find that the first words God ever spoke concerning man were:

"...Let us make man in our image, after our likeness..." (Genesis 1:26).

The only image God ever wanted of Himself is you. This is why Jesus said:

"Ye are the light of the world..." (Matthew 5:14).

Questions to Ponder

1. What is the consequence of making and worshipping images?

2. Why does God hate image worshipping?

3. In what sense are we created in the image and likeness of God?

Holiness: the Crowning Attribute of God

*"And one cried unto another, and said,
Holy, holy, holy, is the LORD of hosts:
the whole earth is full of his glory."*

Isaiah 6:3

Third
Commandment

"I am the LORD thy God...

Thou shalt not take the name of the LORD thy God in vain;

for the LORD will not hold him guiltless that taketh his name in vain."

—Exodus 20:7

This tells us that we must not abuse the name of God. The name of God is to be revered above everything else because God is holy and therefore His name is holy. When Moses first met God, God said to him:

"...Draw not nigh hither: put off thy shoes from off thy feet, for the place whereon thou standest is holy ground. Moreover he said, I am the God of thy father, the God of Abraham, the God of Isaac, and the God of Jacob. And Moses hid

his face; for he was afraid to look upon God" (Exodus 3:5-6).

The Issue of Holiness

In order to understand this commandment, we must understand the concept of holiness. In his first encounter with God, man must know that he is facing a holy God. If a man has not met God in His holiness, then he has not met Him at all. The meeting place of man with God, the innermost chamber of the tabernacle, was called the <u>most holy</u> place. Everything about the Temple, every piece of furniture and every garment of the priest, had to be made holy.

The words *HOLINESS TO THE LORD* were engraved upon the high priest's head band (Exodus 28:36). It was a perpetual reminder that our sins must be dealt with before we can have fellowship with God. Holiness must become a powerful divine principle of every man's being.

When the Prophet Isaiah encountered God in the Temple, he heard seraphim crying to one another:

"Holy, holy, holy, is the LORD of hosts... And the posts of the door moved at the voice of him that cried, and the house was filled with smoke. Then said I, Woe is me! for I am undone..." (Isaiah 6:3-5).

THIRD COMMANDMENT

The word "holiness" and its synonyms occur over 1,000 times in the Holy Bible! The first petition that Jesus bids us to pray in the Lord's Prayer is: *"...Hallowed* [holy] *be thy name"* (Matthew 6:9 [emphasis added]). Jesus' ultimate desire and aspiration for every human being is that we join Him in holiness.

Holiness should be our foremost passion because it is God's supreme desire for all humanity. If we do not seek holiness, we do not seek God - except to use Him to satisfy our earthly desires. If we do not seek holiness, then we have no guarantee that our petitions will be heard by Him when we pray the Lord's Prayer. If we do not seek holiness, we shall not see God:

"Blessed are the pure in heart: for they shall see God" (Matthew 5:8).

"Follow peace with all men, and holiness, without which no man shall see the Lord" (Hebrews 12:14)

As we come to the last book of the Bible, we receive rare insights into the ongoing activity at the throne of God:

"And the four beasts had each of them six wings about him; and they were full of eyes within: and they rest not day and night, saying, Holy,

holy, holy, Lord God Almighty, which was, and is, and is to come" (Revelation 4:8).

The only attribute of God that is lauded over and over again at His throne is His holiness.

Then as we come to the last chapter of the Bible, we have a final confirmation that our destiny depends on us being holy:

"He that is unjust, let him be unjust still: and he which is filthy, let him be filthy still: and he that is righteous, let him be righteous still: and he that is holy, let him be holy still" (Revelation 22:11).

The spiritual condition in which we are living as we arrive at the river of death will be ours forever. There will be no conversions, no make-up time for neglects on earth and no spiritual growth in heaven. We must be holy before we die: *"Because it is written, Be ye holy; for I am holy"* (1 Peter 1:16). Furthermore, holiness is always linked with obedience. It is the way back to the tree of life which Adam abandoned by disobedience. So as disobedience took man out of the Garden of Eden, obedience will take him back into it. All holy people will obey God:

"Blessed are they that do his commandments, that they may have right to the tree of life, and

may enter in through the gates into the city" (Revelation 22:14).

The Holy Name of God

This Third Commandment is an indictment against profanity. It is a clarion call for a clear distinction between the sacred and the profane:

"Thou shalt not take the name of the LORD thy God in vain."

The name of God is holy because God is holy. We must revere His name as much as we revere His person.

While the Second Commandment focuses on doing, this commandment focuses on speaking. Our words are the mirrors of our hearts. James said:

"For in many things we offend all. If any man offend not in word, the same is a perfect man, and able also to bridle the whole body" (James 3:2).

God pays careful attention to what comes out of our mouths. When we speak that which is godly, it will be recorded and reviewed in heaven's library forever. Let us look at this remarkable passage:

"Then they that feared the LORD spake often one to another: and the LORD hearkened,

and heard it, and a book of remembrance was written before him for them that feared the LORD, and that thought upon his name" (Malachi 3:16).

Sometimes religious people justify their misspoken words by saying, "I did not mean to say that." Oh yes you did, for Jesus said:

"...for out of the abundance of the heart the mouth speaketh. A good man out of the good treasure of the heart bringeth forth good things: and an evil man...evil things" (Matthew 12:34-35).

Our speech reveals who and what we are.

Ways We Abuse the Name of God

1. <u>We abuse the name of God when we teach false doctrines claiming that they are of God</u>. Jesus said of the scribes and Pharisees:

"...in vain they do worship me, teaching for doctrines the commandments of men" (Matthew 15:9).

He also warned His disciples to beware of the leaven of the Pharisees (Matthew 16:6), meaning their false doctrines. In Galatians, Paul warns us:

"But though we, or an angel from heaven, preach any other gospel unto you than that

which we have preached unto you, let him be accursed" (Galatians 1:8).

Speaking false doctrines profanes the name of God.

2. <u>We abuse the name of God when we seek self-advantage</u>:

"Not everyone that saith unto me, Lord, Lord, shall enter into the kingdom of heaven; but he that doeth the will of my Father which is in heaven. Many will say to me in that day, Lord, Lord, have we not prophesied in thy name? and in thy name have cast out devils? and in thy name done many wonderful works?" (Matthew 7:21-22).

Those who preach, heal and cast out devils in Jesus' name are not always Jesus' disciples.

The devil can do miracles or counterfeit some of the works of God. For example, the magicians of Egypt transformed rods into serpents as Moses did (Exodus 7:11-12). Jesus prophesied that in the last days there would be many deceivers, and many shall be deceived:

"And many false prophets shall rise, and shall deceive many" (Matthew 24:11).

"Many" could well mean that most prophets and ministers will abuse the name of God in the last days to promote themselves and their religious works. Therefore let us heed these words of Jesus:

"...Every plant, which my heavenly Father hath not planted, shall be rooted up" (Matthew 15:13).

Only what is of the Holy Spirit will last. Only the Holy Spirit can feed us.

3. <u>We abuse the name of God when we try to show off</u>. Often people try to gain spiritual influence over others by parading their spiritual gifts and experiences. The Corinthian Christians had all the gifts, but Paul said that they continued to be carnal (fleshly) and walked as men of the world (1 Corinthians 3:3). The signs of spirituality were not found in them.

Special divine visitations of the Lord are also things for which to praise Him, but they are not given for showmanship. Spiritual gifts are precious, but they in themselves are not proof that a man is walking with God. It is the <u>fruits</u> of the Spirit, not the <u>gifts</u>, that testify that we have been with Jesus (Galatians 5:22-24). Jesus said that you shall know them by their fruits, not by their gifts (Matthew 7:20).

Also, the abundance of miracles done in a church is no proof of her spirituality. Jesus did more miracles in Capernaum than in any other city; yet He said Capernaum was more wicked than

Sodom, and He condemned her to hell (Matthew 11:23). Let us echo the Apostle Paul's great words:

"But God forbid that I should glory, save in the cross of our Lord Jesus Christ, by whom the world is crucified unto me, and I unto the world" (Galatians 6:14).

4. <u>We abuse the name of God when we profess falsely that God has led us</u>. Many churchgoers say, "The Lord told me to marry this person, to buy this home, to go on this journey or to join this church." By saying "The Lord told me...," people build a wall of protection around their "leading." They basically say, "I do not need anyone's advice or opinion. I know what I am doing and I am going to do it." They shut themselves off from the wisdom of the aged, from the knowledge of the holy, from the discernment of the discerners, and from those who are called of God to watch over their souls.

Do not trust "leadings" of people who do not pay their bills, who do not tithe, who are not faithful to their spouses, who have unconfessed sins in their lives, or who fail to show genuine Christlikeness:

"Thou shalt not take the name of the LORD thy God in vain."

5. <u>We abuse the name of God when we claim to be something we are not</u>. When we present

ourselves as Christians, but are far from loving God with all our heart, soul, mind and strength, we are deceived. Jesus said of the religious leaders of His day:

"But woe unto you, scribes and Pharisees, hypocrites! for ye shut up the kingdom of heaven against men: for ye neither go in yourselves, neither suffer [allow] *ye them that are entering to go in"* (Matthew 23:13 [emphasis added]).

"Ye blind guides, which strain at [filter out] *a gnat, and swallow a camel"* (Matthew 23:24 [emphasis added]).

"Woe unto you, scribes and Pharisees, hypocrites! for ye make clean the outside of the cup and of the platter, but within they are full of extortion and excess" (Matthew 23:25).

"Even so ye also outwardly appear righteous unto men, but within ye are full of hypocrisy and iniquity" (Matthew 23:28).

When Christ is busy within us, our profession of faith will match our motives, our passions, our actions and our reactions. We can tell more about a man by his reactions than by almost anything else. When Christ is busy within us, quickening, directing and ever refreshing us, it will show by our works. Of this James said, *"...faith without works is dead"* (James 2:20).

When we partake of the Lord's Supper and have not been following Jesus, we shame the name of God and may be punished by sickness or an untimely death:

"For he that eateth and drinketh unworthily, eateth and drinketh damnation to himself, not discerning the Lord's body. For this cause many are weak and sickly among you, and many sleep" (1 Corinthians 11:29-30).

There are men and women on the sickbed or in the cemetery because they have taken of the Lord's Supper unworthily.

6. We abuse the name of God when we use God's name in an oath. Jesus referred to the Third Commandment when He said:

"But I say unto you, Swear not at all; neither by heaven; for it is God's throne: Nor by the earth; for it is his footstool: neither by Jerusalem; for it is the city of the great King. Neither shalt thou swear by thy head, because thou canst not make one hair white or black. But let your communication be, Yea, yea; Nay, nay: for whatsoever is more than these cometh of evil" (Matthew 5:34-37).

This passage is another call to integrity of speech. Jesus wants us to mean what we say and to say what we mean:

"Thou shalt not take the name of the LORD thy God in vain; for the LORD will not hold him guiltless that taketh his name in vain."

Unbelievers are often careless by abusing the name of God in slang. Expressions like "GEE" or "GEE-WHIZ" derived from Jesus, or "GOSH" and "GOLLY" relating to God, are using the name of God in vain.

This Third Commandment is a call to holiness: in our words, in our lifestyle and in our deeds. To defile, to misrepresent or to abuse the sacred name of God will invite serious consequences. We will not be held guiltless. Since we will be judged for every idle word coming out of our mouths (Matthew 12:36), how much more severe will the judgment be when we profane that Holy Name by which alone we can be saved?

THIRD COMMANDMENT

Questions to Ponder

1. Why is it important to revere God's name?

2. Can we expect to hear God's voice providing us with direction for our lives when we dishonor His holy name?

3. According to the Apostle James, what kind of persons would we be if we would let our voices be the mouth pieces of God (James 3:2)?

The Sabbath: Looking Eternity in the Eye

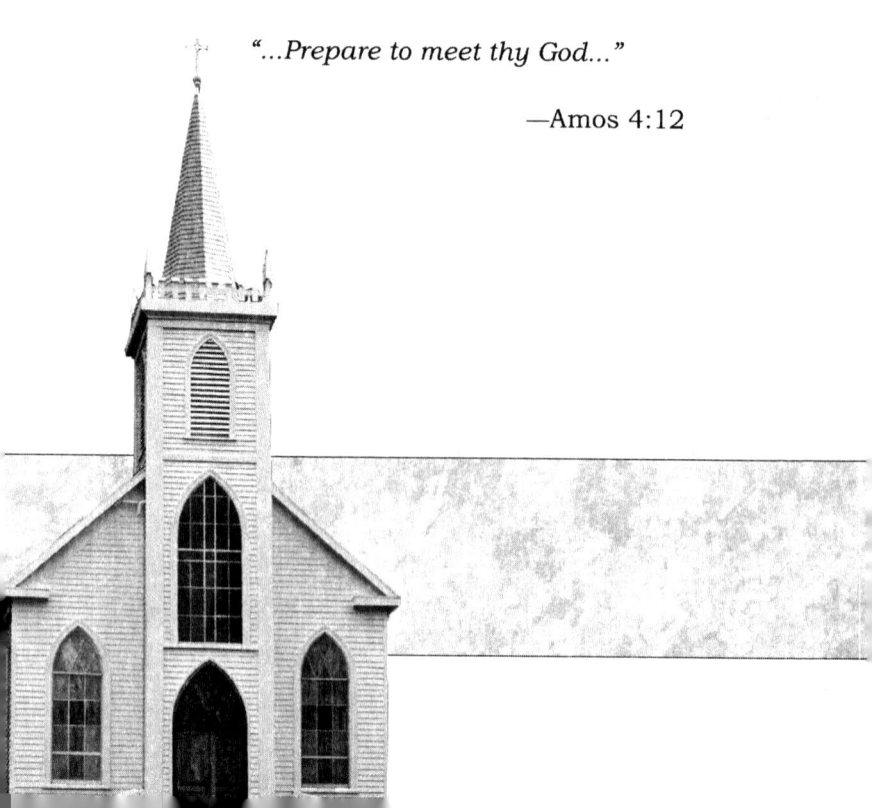

"...Prepare to meet thy God..."

—Amos 4:12

Fourth Commandment

"I am the LORD thy God...

Remember the sabbath day, to keep it holy.

Six days shalt thou labour, and do all thy work: But the seventh day is the sabbath of the LORD thy God: in it thou shalt not do any work, thou, nor thy son, nor thy daughter, thy manservant, nor thy maidservant, nor thy cattle, nor thy stranger that is within thy gates: For in six days the LORD made heaven and earth, the sea, and all that in them is, and rested the seventh day: wherefore the LORD blessed the sabbath day, and hallowed it."

—Exodus 20:8-11

This commandment tells us that the seventh day is the Lord's. This means that it is not ours to do with as we please. It means that when we take the Sabbath away from our Lord, we are thieves and robbers. The Lord has sanctified and blessed this day from the beginning; let us not unsanctify and unbless it by self-indulgence. The Sabbath is a gift from God, a gift of love, a day off from labor for everyone in the house: from the master to the lowest servant, even to the beasts of burden: the oxen, donkeys and horses.

The Origin of the Sabbath

As we come to this commandment, we must realize that there is a distinction to be made between God's laws and Moses' laws. God's laws are the Ten Commandments which were spoken by Him. They were written on tablets of stone and placed in the Ark of the Covenant (Deuteronomy 31:26), suggesting their permanent nature and telling us that they belong in the very heart of man. Then there were the 613 laws of Moses written on paper to guide Israel until her Messiah would come. <u>So it should be noted that the law of the Sabbath is a law of God and not a law of Moses</u>. When you keep it, you are not under Moses' law, but under God's law. This is what the Apostle James meant when he said:

"For whosoever shall keep the whole law, and yet offend in one point, he is guilty of all. For he that said, Do not commit adultery, said also,

Do not kill. Now if thou commit no adultery, yet if thou kill, thou art become a transgressor of the law" (James 2:10-11).

Every one of the Ten Commandments is to be taken as seriously as any other.

Sabbath worship came out of God resting after His creation of the world. And on the Sabbath He wants all of His people to rest with Him.

The Bible teaches that God's people already held the Sabbath dear even before they were forged together into one nation under God at Mount Sinai. In the wilderness, the Sabbath was upheld, though it had not as yet become constitutional law (Exodus 16:23). The Sabbath was given to us so that we could rest and consider eternity. This is the kindness and wisdom of God.

The Sabbath Is a Sacrament

The Sabbath, along with Baptism and Holy Communion, constitute key sacraments of the church. These three ordinances are the visible proofs that identify every Christian as a member of the body of Christ and of the church universal. The Sabbath was the most holy sacrament in the days of the Law, and so it is to be in the age of the Church. The Jews observed it, Jesus observed it and the early Church observed it (Luke 4:16; 1 Corinthians 16:2; Revelation 1:10).

If the head of the house does not keep the Sabbath holy, harmful spiritual influences will begin to bear down upon his family for generations to come through his disobedience. As important as the hub is to the wheel of a bicycle, so the Sabbath is important to the Christian. All the spokes of a bicycle hub run to the rim to hold up the wheel; so all the deeds, actions, decisions and contemplations of the Christian run out of the way he treats the Sabbath. If the Christian does not keep the Sabbath holy, he begins the new week out of tune with God.

Why is it that the church is so weak? Why does the world frequently have more influence on the professing church than the church does on the world? Part of the answer is that many believers are going their own ways, finding their own pleasure, and speaking their own words on that blessed Sabbath day (Isaiah 58:13). If the hub of a wheel is broken, the wagon will not go anywhere.

The Good of the Sabbath

There are two components to this commandment in which all Sabbath teaching is grounded: the first is, "keep it holy;" the second is, "you shall not do any work therein" (Exodus 20:8, 10). If we break either one of these two segments of this law, we are Sabbath-breakers. The Prophet

Isaiah gives further strength and transparency to this law with these words hundreds of years after it was first published:

"If thou turn away thy foot from the sabbath, from doing thy pleasure on my holy day; and call the sabbath a delight, the holy of the LORD, honourable; and shalt honour him, not doing thine own ways, nor finding thine own pleasure, nor speaking thine own words: Then shalt thou delight thyself in the LORD; and I will cause thee to ride upon the high places of the earth, and feed thee with the heritage of Jacob thy father: for the mouth of the LORD hath spoken it" (Isaiah 58:13-14).

Notice the triple prohibitions in reference to the Sabbath here:

- *"not doing thine own ways,"*
- *"nor finding thine own pleasure,"*
- *"nor speaking thine own words."*

Clearly, the Sabbath belongs to the Lord, all of it. It is on this day that the Christian is to spend more time with God and His people than any other day of the week. On this day, he is called upon to worship in the house of God. Worship and tabernacle are linked together in the mind of God. When God gave instruction for the first sanctuary to be built, He said concerning it that it will be:

"...where I will meet with thee: it shall be unto you most holy" (Exodus 30:36).

Likewise Paul admonishes us with these words:

"Not forsaking the assembling of ourselves together, as the manner of some is; but exhorting one another: and so much the more, as ye see the day approaching" (Hebrews 10:25).

Ways of Keeping the Sabbath

1. <u>On this day, the Christian is called upon to lay down his burdens</u>, disengage himself from worldly influences, and also cleanse himself from them:

"Having therefore these promises, dearly beloved, let us cleanse ourselves from all filthiness of the flesh and spirit, perfecting holiness in the fear of God" (2 Corinthians 7:1).

2. <u>On this day, he can examine himself</u> to discover if there is any unforgiving, resentful, critical, prideful, judgmental or self-seeking spirit within him that hinders his fellowship with his Lord:

"Order my steps in thy word: and let not any iniquity have dominion over me" (Psalm 119:133).

FOURTH COMMANDMENT

3. <u>On this day, he can refresh his soul</u> by reviewing what God has done for him and by meditating on His greatness, goodness and mercy:

"I will remember the works of the LORD: surely I will remember thy wonders of old" (Psalm 77:11).

4. <u>On this day, he has extra time to study</u> to show himself *"...approved unto God, a workman that needeth not to be ashamed, rightly dividing the word of truth"* (2 Timothy 2:15).

5. <u>On this day, he must prepare himself for the spiritual warfare lying ahead</u> of him in the coming week:

"Put on the whole armour of God, that ye may be able to stand against the wiles of the devil" (Ephesians 6:11).

6. <u>On this day, the Christian has time for visiting the sick, the needy, the widows and orphans</u>:

"And the King shall answer and say unto them, Verily I say unto you, Inasmuch as ye have done it unto one of the least of these my brethren, ye have done it unto me" (Matthew 25:40).

7. <u>On this day, he is encouraged to give himself to prayer with others in the house of God for the persecuted Christians</u>:

"Remember them that are in bonds, as bound with them; and them which suffer adversity, as being yourselves also in the body" (Hebrews 13:3).

8. <u>On this day, the Christian has the opportunity to strengthen his marriage and to engage himself with his children</u> according to their needs and pleasure in the Lord:

"Lo, children are an heritage of the LORD: and the fruit of the womb is his reward" (Psalm 127:3).

9. <u>This is also a good day for the Christian to connect with God's creation</u> after worship in the house of God:

"The heavens declare the glory of God; and the firmament sheweth his handywork. Day unto day uttereth speech, and night unto night sheweth knowledge" (Psalm 19:1-2).

Rewards for Keeping the Sabbath Holy

Notice the words of reward for the Sabbath keepers from Isaiah 58:13-14:

- Thou shalt delight thyself;
- Thou shalt ride upon the high places;
- Thou shalt be fed.

If we keep the Sabbath holy, God will envelop us with His sweetness and glory. We will ride on His omnipotent strength. We will experience what is most noble, precious and rewarding. If we keep the Sabbath, He will reveal to us *"...the treasures of darkness, and the hidden riches in secret places..."* (Isaiah 45:3). We shall sit with Him in heavenly places with Christ Jesus. God will bless us and our children. He will feed us with bread which is hidden from the world and quench our thirst from the fountain which never runs dry.

The Sabbath Was Made for Man

Yet, we must be careful not to let the Sabbath become an idol, a god to us. We must not worship the Sabbath, but the Lord of the Sabbath. In the history of Israel, from her Babylonian captivity in 600 B.C. to Christ, the Jews became obsessed with the keeping of the Sabbath. They restricted every man by dozens of burdensome laws that dictated what he could and could not do on that day. In fact, the Pharisees tested Jesus as much on His observance of the Sabbath as on His claim of deity.

We must not keep the letter of the law in any commandment to the point where we quench the Spirit of the Lord: *"...for the letter killeth, but the spirit giveth life"* (2 Corinthians 3:6).

In observing the Sabbath day, it helps us to have a sprinkle of sanctified flexibility. For example, acts of mercy were never in violation of the Fourth Commandment. Jesus brought this out plainly when He told the Pharisees that if your sheep falls into a pit on a Sabbath, will you not get him out? He also said that it is right to heal on the Sabbath day; that the Sabbath is for doing good. Ultimately, as Jesus said:

"...The sabbath was made for man, and not man for the sabbath" (Mark 2:27).

Which Day Is the True Sabbath?

Now we come to the question of why Christians predominantly worship God on the first instead of the seventh day of the week, as the Jews had done for centuries. Remember that when Jesus came, He established a new covenant and He ushered in a new kingdom. With that He revealed new doctrines to His precious people - we call them the doctrines of Christ. Prior to this, the Jews had been following the doctrines of Moses. But Jesus came saying, "It has been said by those of old, ...but I say to you..." Paul describes these changes this way:

"Therefore if any man be in Christ, he is a new creature: old things are passed away; behold,

all things are become new" (2 Corinthians 5:17).

Here are a few of the "all things" that are now new:

- The physical temple of old was replaced by a spiritual temple in the heart of man (1 Corinthians 6:19).
- All sacrificing at the temple ceased because Christ became the final sacrifice (Hebrews 7:26-27).
- The ritual requirement for the Jew to be circumcised in the flesh was dropped to make room for the circumcision of the heart toward godliness (Romans 2:29).
- All the Jewish holy days were done away with (Colossians 2:15-17).
- Sunday worship overtook Saturday worship, although not as a result of new doctrinal decrees, but rather as an apostolic preference, to celebrate the resurrection of our Lord (Acts 20:7).

Of course, it was difficult at first for some of the Jewish Christians to be liberated from the laws and practices of Moses. The most difficult things for them to abandon were circumcision, the old dietary laws and the old Sabbath. However, by the end of the first century the practice of Sunday worship was well established. Here are some passages that give credence to the fact that by 100 A.D. the church worshipped on Sundays:

"And upon the first day of the week, when the disciples came together to break bread, Paul preached unto them, ready to depart on the morrow; and continued his speech until midnight" (Acts 20:7).

So here already in about 52 A.D., only 20 years after Christ ascended to heaven, the Christians met on Sunday, the first day of the week, also known as the Lord's Day. As we see from the above verse, there was both preaching and Holy Communion on that day. The following passage indicates that there was also an ingathering of people's tithes and offerings as they came together that day:

"Upon the first day of the week let every one of you lay by him in store, as God hath prospered him, that there be no gatherings when I come" (1 Corinthians 16:2).

Sunday, the Lord's Day, was fully accepted by the Christian community in the second century. This is affirmed by the church leaders who followed

FOURTH COMMANDMENT

after the apostles had gone to heaven. For example, Ignatius in his letter to the Magnesians in about 110 A.D. remarks that those (Jews):

> "...who had lived in antiquated practices came to newness of hope, no longer keeping the Sabbath but living in accordance with the Lord's day, on which our life also arose through Him..."[1]

Justin Martyr (Rome, c. 150) wrote:

> "On the day called Sunday, all who live in cities or in the country gather together in one place, and the memoirs of the apostles or the writings of the prophets are read... Sunday is the day on which we all hold our common assembly, because it is the first day on which God, having wrought a change in the darkness and matter, made the world; and Jesus Christ our Savior on the same day rose from the dead."[2]

However, the "right" day must never become a matter of contention or division for God's blood-cleansed children as Paul mentioned in Romans 14. Even from Jesus, we have the good news that wherever His people gather together, He will be in the midst of them (Matthew 18:20).

Yet, this does not mean that meetings here and there, small or large are acceptable substitutes for the Day of the Lord. God is a jealous God and demands His whole day, each seventh day, on which you must not have your own way, your own pleasure or do any work thereon.

On that day, He wants you and your family to meet with other families to: 1) worship through prayer, praise and song; 2) to come together *"for the perfecting of the saints"* and instructions unto righteousness under the God-ordained, five-fold ministry (Ephesians 4:11-12); 3) to break the bread of life together; 4) to give your tithes and offerings unto the worldwide ministry of the church; and 5) to minister one to another.

God will not absolve you from the Sabbath. It is His day. Do not sell it out to your boss, to the sports, hobby or entertainment gods. If you do so, your spiritual life and that of your family will suffer.

Absolutely, there will not be two heavens, one for the 7th-day and one for the 1st-day worshippers. What is important is that we do recognize one day of the week as the Lord's Day when we come together as the body of Christ saying with the white robed saints in heaven:

"...Alleluia; Salvation, and glory, and honour, and power, unto the Lord our God" (Revelation 19:1).

FOURTH COMMANDMENT

Footnotes:
1 Brace, Robin BD., 2002 "The Early Church Fathers and the Sabbath" UK Apologetics, used with permission: http://www.ukapologetics.net/early/htm

2 Schaff, Phillip (1819-1893) (Editor) "The Apostolic Fathers with Justin Martyr and Irenaeus" Available from: http://www.ccel.org/ccel/schaff/anf01.txt (Public Domain).

Questions to Ponder

1. What is the purpose of the Sabbath?

2. What must we do in order to keep the Sabbath day holy?

3. How does God reward those who keep the Sabbath day holy?

Honoring Father and Mother Has to Be Taught

"Train up a child in the way he should go: and when he is old, he will not depart from it."

—Proverbs 22:6

Fifth Commandment

"I am the LORD thy God...

Honour thy father and thy mother:

that thy days may be long upon the land which the LORD thy God giveth thee."

—Exodus 20:12

Honoring father and mother is man's first responsibility, therefore a child takes his first step towards God when he begins to honor his parents. From the cradle on, a child's destiny is influenced more by how he relates to this commandment than anything else. It is here where the first seeds of human conduct are sown. It is here where the moral compass of a child is set. It is here where the pattern of honoring parents, siblings, schoolteachers, police, elderly, employers, national leaders, and our God will either be established or destroyed. It is also here where foundations for godly character are laid, or it is here where parents begin to allow their child to adopt destructive patterns of self-indulgence. If there is failure here, failure will follow nearly everywhere else. Practically every problem in any nation goes back to parents who have neglected to teach their children to honor authority.

Blessed are the parents who understand from the beginning that a child's obedience is more important than the comforts of life, and that character is more important than education. If every father and mother would raise their children to honor them, to honor their brothers and sisters, to honor their schoolteachers and the laws of the land, divorces would almost come to an end. Police stations would close; prisons would be emptied; industry and government would prosper; and the nation would be blessed beyond measure.

<u>Honoring father and mother does not come naturally; it must be taught</u>. Parents must counter the humanist philosophy of native goodness and realize that deep within every cute and adorable youngster is a sinful nature bent on having his own way. As long as this self-seeking nature is allowed to be the center of the universe, the child is happy. However, whenever the child is

deprived of his wishes, he resorts to an arsenal of disturbing behavior in order to inform his parents of his displeasure. The child may start screaming, pouting, sulking, throwing things or stomping his feet. This pitiful revelation of the true inner nature of a child comes to us not only by observation, but also by the word of God:

"The heart is deceitful above all things, and desperately wicked: who can know it?" (Jeremiah 17:9).

"For from within, out of the heart of men, proceed evil thoughts, adulteries, fornications, murders, Thefts, covetousness, wickedness, deceit, lasciviousness, an evil eye, blasphemy, pride, foolishness: All these evil things come from within, and defile the man" (Mark 7:21-23).

Every new arrival from a mother's womb, without exception, comes into the world with a heart that is wicked, deceitful, evil and defiled. Unless we acknowledge this truth of God Almighty, we are not likely to invest the intense energy, focus, and methods necessary to bring our children into submission to us or to the divine will of God.

Let us now examine four popular methods of child rearing employed today which have miserably failed to satisfy the Fifth Commandment.

Common Methods of Child Rearing

1. <u>Appeasement</u>

The goal of this method is to seek the path of least resistance, to avoid conflict at any cost. From the very start, appeasement will cast to the wind all that is right, noble, and pleasing to God. In most cases of appeasement, the child quickly learns to get the upper hand over his parents as the parents feel an ever-increasing pressure to sacrifice more to keep their child's favor. Before long, the child begins to act as if he is actually the center of the universe. He begins to "parent" his parents, demanding that his parents abandon their schedules for his every whim and wish, utterly exhausting them. Of this, Solomon said:

"...A child left to himself bringeth his mother to shame" (Proverbs 29:15).

2. <u>Reasoning</u>

There are times when it is good to communicate the reasonableness of a command. It shows respect, especially to older children. However, at other times, the parent should be free to not disclose the reason. Some reasons are too heavy for the child to bear or understand. There are also time and environment constraints that dictate whether we choose to explain a command. A child that demands an explanation from his parents before obeying becomes both a judge and a jury. Trying to reason a child into obedience presents these problems:

- Human will is stronger than reason. Once a child has set his mind on something, reason means nothing.

- The child is yet too immature intellectually and emotionally to become a partner in parenting.

- The child will not learn to follow instructions without argumentation, making him unprepared to live in the kingdom of God and the real world.

Can you imagine the chaos if people only obeyed traffic laws, military commands and safety rules after they understood the reasons behind them?

3. Bribery

With bribery, the child will learn that he does not have to do anything without being rewarded. Like someone on drugs, it takes more and more to "buy" the desired behavior. This will not only become very expensive for the parent financially, but it will cost the parent much time and emotional energy. The child will develop an attitude that says, "What will I get out of this? What is in this for me?"

The child will not learn responsibility and the good of serving and sacrificing for others. The child will completely turn inward, seeking nothing but his own gratification. True life is in giving ourselves away to Christ and His beautiful purposes. Jesus said:

"For whosoever will save his life shall lose it: and whosoever will lose his life for my sake shall find it" (Matthew 16:25).

Pampering is not love. It is a sure way to set the child on a path of everlasting ruin, making him difficult to live with, causing problems in the marriage, workplace and with relationships in general.

4. Threats

Threats are worthless unless the punishment follows consistently. When parents do not follow through on their threats, the child quickly learns that such threats are only temper tantrums of frustrated adults, and neither the threats nor his parents are taken seriously. If a threat is not followed through, the parents no longer have credibility and this creates serious insecurity in the child. Be careful to say only what you mean and let that be guided by the Holy Spirit. God never said a word that He did not mean. He never made a promise that He will not keep.

The Biblical Way of Child Rearing

Training is the first Biblical principle of child-rearing. Solomon reminds us that training has long term effects. Without it, children will depart from the way they should go:

"Train up a child in the way he should go: and when he is old, he will not depart from it" (Proverbs 22:6).

This is the only child rearing method with a promise of success.

First, we must make a distinction between teaching, training and discipline. Teaching gives information. It rarely produces desired behavior long-term. However, training develops behavior patterns for the long term. Discipline, which is correction after disobedience, also develops long-term behavior patterns.

The following seven methods of training, although they do not come directly out of specific passages of the Bible, are deeply rooted in biblical principles. Various derivatives of these methods have helped a multitude of parents to raise their children to become notable men and women of God. They are presented to you by one of the author's daughters as a powerful resource, which, if prayerfully applied, can help create positive, productive and godly children in a negative, distorted and ungodly world.[1]

1. <u>Provide your child with positive exposure</u>.

The best setting for successful child rearing is a home full of both love for God, and love and harmony between the husband and wife. In such an environment, your child will learn sacrificial love in the way the father gives himself to the needs of the mother and he will also learn surrender by the way the mother submits herself to the father. As your child learns love and submission in these horizontal relationships, he will learn love and submission in the vertical relationship between man and God.

2. <u>Your child must learn early that he is not the center of the universe</u>.

When babies are first born, they need to become secure in their mother's love. After several days, when they become secure, they must learn that they are not the sun around which the planets orbit, but they are part of a family. If all of their physical needs are met, it is good not to pick them up every time they cry.

3. <u>Your child needs to learn how to rest</u>.

At about 5 months, start holding your child on your lap, not tightly, but loosely, until he stops crying and is quiet for 5 minutes with no toy or entertainment. Slowly, work up to 20 minutes of quiet, adding 5 minutes each week. After that, you will find that your baby can sit peacefully for long periods of time. This is an incredible benefit in many settings, including church and school. It allows parents to take their children almost anywhere instead of frequently needing a babysitter.

4. <u>Your child needs to know the meaning and power of the word "NO."</u>

A very young child can be taught to consistently obey the word "no" in a few days. When you recognize that your child understands "no" (usually at about 5 to 8 months old), it is time to set up training sessions. Put a temptation (eyeglasses, trash can, etc.) in front of him. Remember that God did not put the tree of the knowledge of good and evil in the Garden of Eden up on a shelf. When he reaches for the temptation, thump him lightly on the hand, just enough to sting a little, and quietly say "no." When he tries again, thump his hand again: not hard, but enough to cause a little pain. Repeat until he gives up. Set up several training sessions until a quiet "no" from you is obeyed every time without any physical contact. Yelling is unnecessary and damaging. A quiet "no" is all you need for your child to obey.

5. <u>Your child needs to know the meaning of the word "COME."</u>

Train your child to come immediately when called. This may save his life in an emergency. Allow him to become engrossed in playing with a toy. Call him to come to you with a cheerful voice. If he does not come, either you or someone else should bring him to where you were when you called. Do this twice. The third time, swat him lightly on the leg if he does not come and help him to come. Repeat this exercise until he comes when called. Soon, this pattern will be established for life. Your child will come immediately every time he is called.

6. <u>Your child must know that you love him</u>.

If you discipline your child without giving him love, you drive a wedge between you and your child. The child may submit to you out of fear, but inwardly he will resent you and rebel against you. Discipline without love is destructive. Loving your child includes spending time with him. We cannot win without love:

"He that loveth not knoweth not God; for God is love" (1 John 4:8).

7. <u>Training your child must be reinforced with punishment</u>.

Solomon, the wisest mortal man who ever lived, gave us these thoughts on child rearing:

"He that spareth his rod hateth his son: but he that <u>loveth him</u> chasteneth him betimes" (Proverbs 13:24 [emphasis added]).

"Chasten thy son while there is hope, and let not thy soul spare for his crying" (Proverbs 19:18).

"Foolishness is bound in the heart of a child; but the rod of correction shall drive it far from him" (Proverbs 22:15).

"The rod and reproof give wisdom: but a child left to himself bringeth his mother to shame" (Proverbs 29:15).

"Correct thy son, and he shall give thee rest; yea, he shall give delight unto thy soul" (Proverbs 29:17).

In this context, it should be noted that God is both a loving God and a strict disciplinarian, as emphasized in Hebrews:

"For whom the Lord loveth he chasteneth, and scourgeth every son whom he receiveth" (Hebrews 12:6).

Rather than being cruel, this kind of discipline is of the utmost kindness. Parents demand respect because God says it should be done, not because they are despots. They take care to obey God themselves and they truly believe God's ways will benefit the child the most. The ultimate cruelty is for a father and mother to neglect to instill into their child a submissive and obedient spirit early in life. This neglect will later on bring their child to inner misery and everlasting destruction. The pampered child is doomed to failure in school, jobs, and relationships.

We must understand that every disobedient act dishonors divinely ordained authority. At all costs, the natural predisposition of a child towards the self-life must be reversed. This cannot be accomplished without much effort on our part and strong divine assistance on heaven's part.

At the heart of discipline is that your child's self-will must be broken. Self-will will never take a step after Jesus. This is why Jesus said:

"...If any man will come after me, let him deny himself, and take up his cross daily, and follow me" (Luke 9:23).

Jesus died on His cross to save us, and we have to die on our cross to follow Him. So the purpose of the rod is for the self-will (not the spirit) of your child to become broken and pliable in order to obey God's will.

Of course, discipline must be given to your child in the same manner God disciplines you: not in anger, but with consistency, great love and a firm, but gentle spirit. Carnal tactics never help, but only hinder. We must first be disciplined ourselves before we can give our little ones loving and consistent correction. The punishment must go beyond a slap of a hand, for this will only irritate the child, making him angry at the parent. It must bring the child into a penitent spirit. The cry of the child will change from anger to repentance when discipline is administered correctly. The child is then to be taken into the arms of the parent to be loved and comforted and prayed with because all repentant hearts need the experience of immediate comfort and acceptance.

The child must learn that any disobedience is not worth the effort. In this manner the child is taught to fear the rod, as well as to revere, obey and honor both man and God (1 Peter 2:17). The child will soon come to be a joy and an ornament of grace to his father and mother. A properly disciplined child loves and cherishes his parents and will naturally honor the elderly, governmental powers and all those who have authority over us in our places of service or work (1 Timothy 5:1; Romans 13:1-2; Ephesians 6:5-8, 1 Peter 2:17).

Any submission to God's ordained authority is part of our service and submission to the Lord. Joseph submitted to all authority and because of his submission, he was eventually promoted to become the Prime Minister of Egypt. Honoring authority invariably brings a godly countenance upon the faces of His people, causing them to rise from the pit to the palace. How far our children will rise to places of honor very much depends on what we, as parents, put into them early in life.

If these particular admonitions are followed, there will be fruits abounding. Christianity begins with submission. This is what we are admonished to do in the Fifth Commandment, and if we do it well, it will be well with us. Everything else will flow out of this. If we fail to discipline our children, we will deprive them of the joy of the Lord which is our strength (Nehemiah 8:10).

Finally, it is important to understand that training and conversion are two different things. Training is the work of man preparing the child to walk with God. Conversion is the work of the Holy Spirit giving our children a heart after God's own heart to live with Him forever.

"Honour thy father and thy mother..."

"Honour all men... Fear God. Honour the king" (1 Peter 2:17).

Footnotes:

1 Morey, Esther (Pamphlet) "The Lamb Will Rule, Not the Lion"

Questions to Ponder

1. What will God think of us if we allow our children to develop behavior patterns and habits that later must be broken?

2. To what does Samuel relate rebellion? (1 Samuel 15:23)

3. What price are you willing to pay to train your child to walk with God?

Murder Begins with Irreverence to God

*"The fear of the LORD tendeth to life:
and he that hath it shall abide satisfied;
he shall not be visited with evil."*

—Proverbs 19:23

Sixth Commandment

"I am the LORD thy God...

Thou shalt not kill."
—Exodus 20:13

The Third Commandment teaches us to revere God. This commandment teaches us to revere man. We learn to revere man by revering God, the giver of all life. All abuses of man against man come out of irreverence toward God.

Here Are Three Biblical Reasons Why We Need to Revere Man:

1. <u>We must revere man because he is created in the image of God</u>.

From creation, God and man have been linked together. The marvel of the gospel is that God not only reveres man in perfection, but also in imperfection, for the Scriptures say:

"But God commendeth his love toward us, in that, while we were yet sinners, Christ died for us" (Romans 5:8).

2. <u>We must revere man because God endowed him with an eternal soul</u>.

Of all God has created in the heavens above, and the earth and seas below, man will be the only survivor at the end of the age. Everything else will be destroyed, as the Apostle Peter attests:

"Looking for and hasting unto the coming of the day of God, wherein the heavens being on fire shall be dissolved, and the elements shall melt with fervent heat? Nevertheless we, according to his promise, look for new heavens and a new earth, wherein dwelleth righteousness" (2 Peter 3:12-13).

This means that at the end of time men will either be raised to eternal life or to eternal damnation. Our Lord said:

"Marvel not at this: for the hour is coming, in the which all that are in the graves shall hear his voice, And shall come forth; they that have done good, unto the resurrection of life; and they that have done evil, unto the resurrection of damnation" (John 5:28-29).

Man has an eternal, indestructible soul.

3. <u>We must revere man because he was created to become the bride of Christ</u>:

"And I heard as it were the voice of a great multitude, and as the voice of many waters, and as the voice of mighty thunderings, saying, Alleluia: for the Lord God omnipotent reigneth. Let us be glad and rejoice, and give honour to him: for the marriage of the Lamb is come, and his wife hath made herself ready" (Revelation 19:6-7).

Man was created for heaven to sit with Jesus in His throne:

"To him that overcometh will I grant to sit with me in my throne, even as I also overcame, and am set down with my Father in his throne" (Revelation 3:21).

For these three reasons, the Bible holds us to a high standard of love towards all men, to the extent that John tells us that if we do not love man, neither do we love God:

"If a man say, I love God, and hateth his brother, he is a liar: for he that loveth not his brother whom he hath seen, how can he love God whom he hath not seen?" (1 John 4:20).

The Origin of Irreverence to Man

The first picture of man's inhumanity to his

fellow man is seen when the first man born of woman, Cain, murdered his brother Abel. Cain lost reverence to God before he lost reverence to his brother. Both were supposed to give a blood sacrifice to the Lord. However, Cain decided to offer a grain sacrifice instead and his disobedient heart bred resentment, jealousy, hate and murder towards his brother. It all began with his irreverence to God. Cain did not revere God enough to obey Him. Irreverence to God always leads to disobedience on every level.

Violations of the Sixth Commandment

1. <u>Abortion</u>

Many believe that life begins at conception, but the Bible says we existed in the mind of God before there were stars in the heavens and fish in the sea. The Apostle Paul said:

"According as he hath chosen us in him before the foundation of the world, that we should be holy and without blame before him in love" (Ephesians 1:4).

Not only were we chosen before creation, we also were assigned our life's work before God separated light from darkness:

"For we are his workmanship, created in Christ Jesus unto good works, which God hath

SIXTH COMMANDMENT

before ordained that we should walk in them" (Ephesians 2:10).

Everything God created has a divine purpose and plan for the duration of its existence. God planned a specific spouse for us before we were born. Before He said, *"Let there be stars also,"* our place of residence and unique calling were also laid out (Acts 17:26). We are to come before our Lord in everything relating to our life choices since we are not our own (1 Corinthians 6:19b). This is why Jesus has taught us to pray: *"Thy will be done."* All our steps should be ordered by the Lord (Psalm 37:23; Proverbs 16:9). In short, we were conceived in the mind of God before we were conceived in our mother's womb. God said of Jeremiah:

"Before I formed thee in the belly I knew thee; and before thou camest forth out of the womb I sanctified thee, and I ordained thee a prophet unto the nations" (Jeremiah 1:5 [emphasis added]).

Before Jeremiah was conceived in the womb, God knew him, God had sanctified him, and God ordained him to be a prophet.

Hence, abortion is destroying God's dream, God's plan, and God's person. It is taking a life out of God's hands. It is murder. So there is a divine conception, and there is a human conception. Any society that does not recognize the unalienable right of every person to be born is under the judgment of God.

2. <u>Suicide and Euthanasia</u>

Anyone who is sound in faculty of mind and takes his own life is violating this law of God. Euthanasia (assisted suicide) is also a violation of the law of God. Consider these two points why suicide is wrong: God gives life, and He is the only one who has the right to end it:

"And as it is appointed unto men once to die, but after this the judgment" (Hebrews 9:27).

Just as God has appointed a time and place for birth, so He has appointed a time for death:

"To every thing there is a season, and a time to every purpose under the heaven: A time to be born, and a time to die..." (Ecclesiastes 3:1-2).

To pray people beyond their appointed time of death is selfish, irresponsible and faithless. God makes no mistakes. He made no mistake for the time of our birth and He will make no mistake for the time of our death. For those who are in great suffering, death sometimes refuses to come when it is most welcome. But God's ways are higher than ours:

"O the depth of the riches both of the wisdom

and knowledge of God! how unsearchable are his judgments, and his ways past finding out!" (Romans 11:33).

Suicide is wrong because it makes us get ahead of God. Solomon warns us:

"Be not over much wicked, neither be thou foolish: why shouldest thou die before thy time?" (Ecclesiastes 7:17).

If we appoint the day of our death, we take judgment out of the hands of God, making ourselves judges over life and death. This is being overly wicked.

Suicide and euthanasia are wrong because they are the fruits of unbelief. Only unbelievers give up on God. To the believer, God's grace is sufficient and abounding in all circumstances of life. Unbelief is dangerous. We must be faithful (full of faith) to the end. Jesus said:

"...but he that endureth to the end shall be saved" (Matthew 10:22).

"He that believeth on him is not condemned: but he that believeth not is condemned already..." (John 3:18).

In saying *"Thou shalt not kill,"* God laid down the law 3,000 years ago protecting man at the beginning of life and also at the end of life. God says "No" to abortion. God says "No" to murder. God says "No" to suicide. God says "No" to euthanasia.

To commit suicide is the most selfish thing a person can do. For by doing it, a person not only takes his own life out of the hands of God, but he also leaves unending sorrow and pain to his family and friends that will be carried into the next generation and beyond. Suicide never solves a problem. Families who have a suicidal death among them need much love from the body of Christ in order to heal.

Suicide and euthanasia oppose everything Christianity stands for.

3. <u>War</u>

To understand how war relates to this commandment, we need to understand that there are two kingdoms. There is the kingdom of God and the kingdom of man. Jesus said:

"My kingdom is not of this world: if my kingdom were of this world, then would my servants fight, that I should not be delivered to the Jews: but now is my kingdom not from hence" (John 18:36).

In Christ's kingdom, the weapons of our warfare are spiritual:

"For though we walk in the flesh, we do not war after the flesh: For the weapons of our warfare

are not carnal, but mighty through God to the pulling down of strong holds" (2 Corinthians 10:3-4).

"Put on the whole armour of God, that ye may be able to stand against the wiles of the devil. For we wrestle not against flesh and blood, but against principalities, against powers, against the rulers of the darkness of this world, against spiritual wickedness in high places. Wherefore take unto you the whole armour of God..." (Ephesians 6:11-13).

Although Jesus told Peter to put away the sword, He did not tell Rome to do likewise. Rather, He speaks through Paul saying that all civil powers are of God and have the right to bear arms:

"...For there is no power but of God: the powers that be are ordained of God" (Romans 13:1).

"For he is the minister of God to thee for good. But if thou do that which is evil, be afraid; for he beareth not the sword in vain: for he is the minister of God, a revenger to execute wrath upon him that doeth evil" (Romans 13:4).

Civil authorities have the right to use the sword.

Jesus and the Sixth Commandment

In the Sermon on the Mount, Jesus once again takes us deeper than Moses ever did:

"Ye have heard that it was said by them of old time, Thou shalt not kill; and whosoever shall kill shall be in danger of the judgment: But I say unto you, That whosoever is angry with his brother without a cause shall be in danger of the judgment..." (Matthew 5:21-22).

Here Jesus takes us to the root of murder. All murder is birthed in resentment, anger and hatred. This gets us back again to our Lord's words:

"For out of the heart proceed evil thoughts, murders, adulteries, fornications, thefts, false witness, blasphemies" (Matthew 15:19).

This means that although we may not kill people physically, we can destroy them through our anger: by criticizing them, by destroying their reputation, or through depriving them of what they need when it is in our power to help them.

Jesus told us to love both our brothers and our enemies. Our love to God is never greater than our love to our worst enemy. Let Jesus take residence in our hearts and we shall fulfill this commandment: *"Thou shalt not kill."* Killing begins with irreverence to God.

Finally, can a murderer be forgiven? Yes, he certainly can. The most influential man of the Old Testament, Moses, was a murderer (Exodus 2:11-12). He was forgiven, mightily used of God and privileged to see Jesus in His celestial glory on the Mount of Transfiguration. The most influential man since Jesus, the Apostle Paul, was responsible for the death of many Christians (Acts 26:10). He was forgiven to become a shining jewel in the Master's crown:

"Wherefore he is able also to save them to the uttermost that come unto God by him, seeing he ever liveth to make intercession for them" (Hebrews 7:25).

Questions to Ponder

1. Why must we revere man?

2. How did Jesus show His reverence to man?

3. What role does reverencing man play in evangelism?

Marriage: a Prototype of Christ and His Church

"What therefore God hath joined together, let no man put asunder."

—Mark 10:9

Seventh Commandment

"I am the LORD thy God...

Thou shalt not commit adultery.
—Exodus 20:14

This commandment is given to preserve the sanctity of marriage. Adultery is breaking the law in that it breaks the marriage vow. Adultery breaks the heart of God. This doctrine: *"What therefore God hath joined together, let no man put asunder [separate]"* (Mark 10:9 [emphasis added]), has been undisputed for most of the church age. The Catholic Church still adheres to it and so does a good part of the Protestant church.

What Is Adultery?

- Adultery is a sexual relationship between a married person and someone who is not their spouse.

"...Whosoever shall put away his wife, and marry another, committeth adultery against her. And if a woman shall put away her husband, and be married to another, she committeth adultery" (Mark 10:11-12).

- Adultery is marrying someone who is divorced whose spouse is still living.

"Whosoever putteth away his wife, and marrieth another, committeth adultery: and whosoever marrieth her that is put away from her husband committeth adultery" (Luke 16:18).

These teachings come from the lips of our Lord Jesus Christ in the gospels:

"...What therefore God hath joined together, let not man put asunder" (Matthew 19:6).

Under Old Testament law, adultery was deserving of death (Deuteronomy 22:22). Under New Testament teachings, adulterers are excluded from the kingdom of God:

"For this ye know, that no whoremonger [adulterous person], *...hath any inheritance in the kingdom of Christ and of God"* (Ephesians 5:5 [emphasis added]).

Let us now consider why the breakup of a marriage is such a serious matter. All theology must begin with us looking to God. Marriage came from the mind of God.

Marriage: A Picture of the Divine Romance

To understand why God is so zealous to guard marriage, we have to go back to some point in eternity when all members of the Holy Trinity expressed their intense desire for a bride for the Son of God. With this in mind, we can imagine these three Divine Persons saying in a chorus of absolute harmony and superlative ecstasy:

"...Let us make man in our image, after our likeness..." (Genesis 1:26).

Through these vital words, the whole purpose of the universe was made known: the earth is to serve as a temporary dwelling place to prepare man to become the bride of Christ. At the end of the age, man will then be joined forever with Jesus in the great marriage supper of the Lamb. So as the crowning work of creation, God established the union of a man and a woman as the prototype of the divine, inseparable romance between Christ and His church.

Paul explains this parallelism in his Ephesian letter. He describes the husband as a type of Christ, and the wife as a type or example of the church (Ephesians 5:22-25). And because God Himself has put husband and wife together to reflect His own union with the Church, every marriage becomes an anointed threesome. This is why when a marriage is broken up, it breaks up a trinity of three persons. The result is not only a breakup of the relationship between a man and a woman, but also a breakup of a relationship with God for one or both parties. It is for this reason that remarriage when the first spouse is still living, is like defacing a beautiful work of art, destroying its original design beyond recognition. The picture of unconditional love, patience and forgiveness from our Lord toward His wayward bride is gone. This is why a Jewish scholar said: "When a man divorces his first wife, even the altar sheds tears."[1]

Whenever a journey towards adultery begins, self-gratification is chosen over holiness and self-will over God's will by one or both parties. Spiritual blindness sets in and the world loses a living example of the relationship between Christ and His church.

God's Love Affair with Israel

In the Old Testament, we see God in a love affair with Israel, His chosen people. In fact, we see God as being married to Israel. He says to her:

"For thy Maker is thine husband; the LORD of hosts is his name; and thy Redeemer the Holy One of Israel..." (Isaiah 54:5).

But Israel commits adultery. She gives herself

SEVENTH COMMANDMENT 117

entirely to harlotry. How does God respond? He divorces her:

"And I saw, when for all the causes whereby backsliding Israel committed adultery I had put her away, and given her a bill of divorce; yet her treacherous sister Judah feared not, but went and played the harlot also" (Jeremiah 3:8).

Yet, here we learn this astonishing truth: to God, divorce is not the end of marriage and it certainly is not the right to remarry. In fact, notice that God lovingly and firmly scolds His beloved for her iniquities. Then He pleads with her, the divorced one, to repent and to come back to Him. He says to her with great longing:

"...thou hast played the harlot with many lovers; yet return again to me, saith the LORD" (Jeremiah 3:1).

"Turn, O backsliding children, saith the LORD; for I am married unto you and I will bring you to Zion" (Jeremiah 3:14).

These passages lead us to the inevitable conclusion that is so foreign to our thinking, namely that to God, a man can be married and divorced at the same time. Even though God had issued Israel a bill of divorce, He remained committed to His marriage with her, totally dismissing the idea that He would ever look for another bride by saying:

"Behold, I have graven thee upon the palms of my hands; thy walls are continually before me" (Isaiah 49:16).

Finally, although marriage after divorce (when the first spouse is still living) may have social legitimacy through our civil courts, it has no spiritual legitimacy before God. This means divorce does not make a man single again.

Jesus' Teachings on Marriage

In Matthew 19:3-10, Jesus gives us the key to understand His most comprehensive teaching on marriage. These verses also contain the "exception clause" that people use to justify remarriage after divorce. In this cardinal teaching on divorce and remarriage, our Lord moves the church from a full-tolerance doctrine under Moses to a no-tolerance doctrine under His Lordship. It reflects His relationship with His wife, Israel. He provides no exceptions, no excuses, and no escape clauses. Following are the verses from Matthew on divorce which include verse 9 with the popular, but much misunderstood, exception clause:

3 "The Pharisees also came unto him, tempting him, and saying unto him, Is it lawful for a man

SEVENTH COMMANDMENT

to put away his wife for every cause?

4 And he answered and said unto them, Have ye not read, that he which made them at the beginning made them male and female,

5 And said, For this cause shall a man leave father and mother, and shall cleave [be joined inseparably] *to his wife: and they twain* [two] *shall be one flesh?*

6 Wherefore they are no more twain, but one flesh. What therefore God hath joined together, let not man put asunder.

7 They say unto him, Why did Moses then command [allow] *to give a writing of divorcement, and to put her away?*

8 He saith unto them, Moses because of the hardness of your hearts suffered you to put away your wives: but from the beginning it was not so.

9 And I say unto you, Whosoever shall put away his wife, except it be for fornication, and shall marry another, committeth adultery: and whoso marrieth her which is put away doth commit adultery.

10 His disciples say unto him, If the case of the man be so with his wife, it is not good to marry" (Matthew 19:3-10 [emphasis added]).

Let us divide this passage into four sections to better understand the main points Jesus made.

1. <u>Two persons become one in marriage</u>.

In verses 4-6, Jesus begins His discourse on marriage by deriding the Pharisees for their ignorance or neglect in comprehending the significance of Genesis 2:24. With these verses, Jesus lays down the foundation in which all discussions on marriage and divorce must be grounded: namely, that in marriage the husband and wife are divinely joined together to form a union of one flesh, becoming as one person that no man has authority to divide. This means that God will not approve of anyone entering a second marriage while the first spouse is still living.

2. <u>Jesus dismisses the teachings of Moses on marriage because they do not fit the Messianic Age</u>.

In verses 7 and 8, Jesus totally dismisses Moses' permissive laws on remarriage since they were not founded on God's original intent. Moses allowed these divorce procedures because of the hardness of the peoples' hearts, but now Jesus is here. Jesus now moves the church from the former loose accommodating laws of Moses to a superior system reflecting His own relationship with His spouse.

3. <u>Jesus allows divorce in the case of fornication</u>.[2]

In verse 9, Jesus declares that any person who divorces his wife and marries another commits adultery. With these words, Jesus protects and preserves marriage. Jesus says that a man is justified to divorce his wife if she commits fornication. Still, He does not endorse the right of remarriage for either party because <u>although they are divorced, they are still one flesh, one person</u>. Again, with God, divorce does not end a marriage. If the adulteress remarries, she is still one flesh with her first husband. If the man who divorced her remarries, he is still one flesh with his first wife, which puts him also into adultery. The modern idea that this "exception clause" permits remarriage has no validity because the "one flesh" clause overrides it. What God has put together, no man has authority to separate.

It is also worth noting that sexual immorality seldom happens without some failure of both parties. The neglect of love from one party can contribute to the weakness of the other to resist temptation.

4. <u>The disciples were disappointed</u>.

In verse 10, the disciples were so shattered by the stringent teaching of Jesus that they were dismayed, wanting to give up on marriage altogether. We still have many "disciples" who find this teaching too hard, so they become loophole-seekers. Let us beware of a loophole mentality. It will make us miss the fullness of what God has for us. Jesus said the way to life is narrow "...*and few there be that find it*" (Matthew 7:14).

Again, in this teaching, Jesus affirms the authority of Genesis 2:24 on all matters of marriage. This is the foundation of all apostolic teaching on marriage as well. Can we and will we accept this? God made no exit from a marriage but by death.

The Sermon on the Mount and Adultery

"Thou shalt not commit adultery."

Let us now consider that man never knew the depth of this command until Jesus brought it to light in His Sermon on the Mount 2,000 years ago. Here, our Messiah explains that God is not only appalled at physical, but also at spiritual adultery:

"Ye have heard that it was said by them of old time, Thou shalt not commit adultery: But I say unto you, That whosoever looketh on a woman to lust after her hath committed adultery with her already in his heart" (Matthew 5:27-28).

Adultery begins in the heart. Jesus also said:

"For out of the heart proceed evil thoughts, murders, adulteries, fornications..." (Matthew 15:19).

If there is an adulterous spirit in the heart, then an adulterous look will follow. The first look becomes a second look, a third look and so on.

When it comes to adultery, we are dealing with a heart-eye connection. But the heart that loves God fervently will make no room for the adulterous spirit. It "abides in Christ" and that means it makes its residence in Christ as a branch abides in the vine (John 15:1-7). This intimacy with Jesus comes out of self-denial, obedience and following.

We Abide in Christ by Keeping These Essentials:

1. <u>Reading the Word of God every day</u> to meditate on its truths and inspirations (Psalm 1:2; 2 Timothy 2:15).

2. <u>Praying without ceasing</u> and bringing our praises, supplications, and requests to Christ daily (Psalm 34:1).

3. <u>Witnessing at every opportunity</u> when the Lord leads (Revelation 12:11).

4. <u>Obeying the Word of God and the leadings of the Holy Spirit</u> continually. If we will do so, He will direct our paths (Proverbs 3:5-6). As we obey, we find that the joy of the Lord is our strength

(Nehemiah 8:10). This joy is a gift from God to every obedient heart and with it God will send grace for the moment and strength for the hour.

Through intimacy which is maintained by these four essentials, we shall be more than conquerors through Christ who loves us (Romans 8:37).

"For the weapons of our warfare are not carnal, but mighty through God to the pulling down of strong holds" (2 Corinthians 10:4).

Let us look at two of the greatest men of the Bible as they were tempted by beautiful women: David and Joseph. One's fall and the other's triumph were predetermined by each one's spiritual state before he was tempted.

David started his day with his own desires in the wrong place, complacent and unarmed. He refused to go into the battle to which God had sent him. Instead, he was indulging himself at his palace, so he was unfit to resist the temptation to lust after Bathsheba.

Joseph started his day dressed in the armor of God. He was spiritually prepared, doing exactly what he was assigned to do. Therefore, unlike David who ran towards the temptation, Joseph ran away from it. How we start the day influences how we end it.

The Apostle Paul's Teaching on Marriage

From text and context, we affirm the "except for fornication" clause does NOT point forward to remarriage, but rather it points to the ONLY excuse for divorce. God hates divorce (Malachi 2:16). Again, on the basis of Genesis 2:24, God forbids remarriage while the first spouse is still living. Paul accepted the "one flesh doctrine" of the Lord Jesus. Here he made it the key for his position on the indissolubility of marriage:

"So ought men to love their wives as their own bodies. He that loveth his wife loveth himself. For no man ever yet hated his own flesh; but nourisheth and cherisheth it, even as the Lord the church" (Ephesians 5:28-29).

"For the woman which hath an husband is bound by the law to her husband so long as he liveth; but if the husband be dead, she is loosed from the law of her husband. So then if, while her husband liveth, she be married to another man, she shall be called an adulteress: but if her husband be dead, she is free from that law; so that she is no adulteress, though she be married to another man" (Romans 7:2-3).

Again, clearly the teaching of Jesus applies here: as long as both parties live, whatever the marital difficulties may be, they are one flesh, one person; and divorce will not change that. Paul continues on this subject in his Corinthian letter saying:

> *"And unto the married I command, yet not I, <u>but the Lord</u>, Let not the wife depart from her husband: But and if she depart, <u>let her remain unmarried, or be reconciled to her husband</u>: and let not the husband put away* [divorce] *his wife"* (1 Corinthians 7:10-11 [emphasis added]).

"Reconciliation" means restoration of the first marriage after repentance has been made, if possible.

Paul also makes allowance for separation or divorce, but not remarriage, in case an unbeliever wants to depart from the believer. Speaking out of his apostolic office, he says:

> *12 "But to the rest speak I, not the Lord: If any brother hath a wife that believeth not, and she be pleased to dwell with him, let him not put her away.*

> *13 And the woman which hath an husband that believeth not, and if he be pleased to dwell with her, let her not leave him.*

> *14 For the unbelieving husband is sanctified by the wife, and the unbelieving wife is sanctified*

by the husband: else were your children unclean; but now are they holy.

15 But if the unbelieving depart, let him depart. A brother or a sister is not under bondage [bound to the other] *in such cases: but God hath called us to peace"* (1 Corinthians 7:12-15 [emphasis added]).

Again, the "one flesh" clause applies here. If the husband divorces his wife, either because of fornication or because she chooses to leave, he has two options:

1. To be reconciled to his wife;
2. To remain single as long as she lives.

Divorce in the case of adultery is not a sin, but remarriage while the first spouse is still living is.

One question is, can a divorced mother and her children have their needs met without remarriage? What God said to Paul, He said to all of us:

"...My grace is sufficient for thee: for my strength is made perfect in weakness..." (2 Corinthians 12:9).

And what Paul said to the Philippians, he also said to all of us who are faithful:

"But my God shall supply all your need according to his riches in glory by Christ Jesus" (Philippians 4:19).

Building an Adultery-Proof Marriage

To protect our marriages from breaking up, there are two cardinal rules to be passionately observed:

1. *"Husbands, love your wives, even as Christ also loved the church, and gave himself for it; ...let every one of you in particular so love his wife even as himself..."* (Ephesians 5:25, 33).

2. *"Wives, submit yourselves unto your own husbands, as unto the Lord. ...in every thing. ...and the wife see that she reverence* [respect] *her husband"* (Ephesians 5:22-24, 33 [emphasis added]).

The key for the husband's love towards his wife is in the words, "even as Christ." Christ loves the church <u>as she is</u>. Despite all her spots, wrinkles and blemishes, a wife must be loved unconditionally. A husband is to love his wife as much <u>as he loves himself</u> (Ephesians 5:33). It is in this way that his marriage will be as wonderful in old age as it was in his youth. Solomon describes how this love is one of the greatest wonders, both at the beginning and at the end of life:

"There be three things which are too wonderful for me, yea, four which I know not: The way of an eagle in the air; the way of a serpent upon a rock; the way of a ship in the midst of

the sea; and the way of a man with a maid" (Proverbs 30:18-19).

Man is to enjoy the wife of his youth all the days of his life. This love must always be looked upon as a commitment; it must never come to rest on the ups and downs of feelings. When Jesus asked us to love Him, He did not ask for a feeling, but for a commitment to a relationship.

No matter how great a man's ministry in the eyes of the church, it can be said that if the man does not love his wife, the Spirit of the Lord has departed from him.

The woman's submission to the husband in everything is to be <u>as the submission of the church</u> to Christ in everything. This is not a matter of him being more worthy than she. Both are equally joint heirs with Christ (1 Peter 3:7), but each has a different assignment in the institutions of marriage and family. So if a woman raises her head above that of her husband, she loses the favor of God because she steps out of God's design for the marriage. A well-loved wife will not find this admonition to respect her husband to be a hardship. In addition, by respecting her husband, she will teach her children to honor their parents.

One reason why our churches are so unattractive, especially to young people, is because husbands and wives do not observe these marital admonitions.

Adultery Is Not an Unpardonable Sin

If you have committed adultery, do not despair. Jesus did not come to condemn the world, but to save it. The Pharisees of that day had no mercy for adulterers. But Jesus was merciful in saying:

"I came not to call the righteous, but sinners to repentance" (Luke 5:32).

When Jesus was confronted with an adulterous woman, His message to her was:

"...Neither do I condemn thee: go, and sin no more" (John 8:11).

Jesus calls every adulterer to holiness of life.

Because of the permissive marriage laws in the days of Jesus among both the Jews and Romans, the remarriage rate amongst divorcees was very high. It is likely that the early church had more former adulterers as converts than at any other time in history. This abundance of people who had come out of an adulterous relationship to receive the Lord Jesus is hinted at by Paul:

"And such were some of you: but ye are washed, but ye are sanctified, but ye are justified in the name of the Lord Jesus, and by the Spirit of our God" (1 Corinthians 6:11).

Through this we see that Jesus wants us to know the depths of His love and mercy that are able to save to the uttermost (Hebrews 7:25). Without that mercy, none of us could be saved.

Although adultery's roots are deeper and its tentacles reach further than those of most other sins, it is forgivable. There is full forgiveness and peace with God to those who confess it, repent of it and make restitution as the Holy Spirit directs. <u>There will be no peace with God for those who justify it</u>.

Finally, although adultery is forgivable, God cares about credentials. As He required high credentials for those who ministered in the temple in days of old, so He does for those who take leadership of a church today. In Paul's letter to Timothy, these credentials are listed, among others:

"A bishop then must be blameless, the husband of one wife, vigilant, sober, of good behaviour, given to hospitality, apt to teach" (1 Timothy 3:2).

Do not commit adultery. When we commit adultery, we not only violate a law, but also the Spirit of God. Jesus said so; an apostle wrote it down. It is church doctrine.

A SPECIAL MESSAGE TO MINISTERS OF TODAY

The church of Jesus Christ must be made keenly aware of the following things:

1. Neglecting to teach these truths about adultery will only guarantee more, successive, adulterous generations. Every young couple needs to know these truths before they get married.

2. Preachers must be delivered from the fear of losing people in their churches by preaching this. It is no kindness for ministers to ignore sins in the people that will bring them to everlasting doom.

3. The church must protect offenders from the harshness of today's Pharisees as Jesus did, and deal with each transgressor with redemptive love.

Adulterers, once forgiven, must forgive themselves and stop dwelling on what they were and begin to focus on what they are now in Christ Jesus.

Footnotes:
1 Taken from the Jewish New Testament Commentary by David H. Stern, Copyright © 1989. All rights reserved. Used by permission of Messianic Jewish Publishers, 6120 Day Long Lane, Clarksville, MD 21029. www.messianicjewish.net. (p. 59).

2 "Fornication" is used in the Bible to include any kind of sexual immorality.

Questions to Ponder

1. What is adultery?

2. As Christ has been long-suffering, forgiving and patient towards you, what do the following scriptures teach you about your need to be forgiving and patient towards others (Matthew 6:14-15; Matthew 18:21-22; Ephesians 4:2, 32)?

3. What are the four essentials for abiding in Christ and in what way do they guard a marriage?

Before We Steal from Man, We Steal from God

"And when the woman saw that the tree was good for food, and that it was pleasant to the eyes... she took of the fruit thereof, and did eat..."

Genesis 3:6

Eighth Commandment

"I am the LORD thy God...

Thou shalt not steal."
—Exodus 20:15

WE steal when we are not content with what God has given us to be stewards over. The root of every theft is discontentment. People who are content with what they have do not steal:

"But godliness with contentment is great gain" (1 Timothy 6:6).

The Origin of Stealing

We learned earlier that once man was placed in the garden of God, God entered into a legal relationship with him, to bless and protect him. Man's side of the contract was prefaced by these words: *"thou mayest"* and *"thou shalt not"* (Genesis 2:16-17).

However, a relationship preceded that contract: the owner/steward relationship (Genesis 1:28, 2:15). That is the beginning of man's responsibility to God. We must understand the primacy of this owner/steward relationship in order to have correct doctrines and theology. God is the absolute sovereign Lord and we are His stewards. We will be held accountable for what we have done with our stewardship on that great Judgment Day, when all the books will be opened and we will be judged according to the works we have done (Revelation 20:12).

Here are God's first words to man:

"...Be fruitful, and multiply, and replenish the earth, and subdue it: and have dominion over the fish of the sea..." (Genesis 1:28).

Notice some of the things we can gather from God's first words to man:

- God as owner tells man what to do. God telling man what to do, and man doing it is what Christianity is all about. It is what your daily life is meant to be all about. If you don't have a life like that, you don't have God. From the very beginning no allowance was made for man to do what he wanted to do. Jesus put this in His prayer for us by telling us to pray: *"Thy will be done."*

EIGHTH COMMANDMENT

- God expresses incredible trust in man. He essentially says to Adam: "I trust you with all the earth. I believe you are able to be a good steward over all of it." This deep trust of God in man comes out of His deep love for him.

- By implication, and scattered throughout the whole Bible, is the doctrine that man will have to give an account of his stewardship.

- In this passage we see a pattern of what all owner/stewardship relationships are to be like. We see a picture of a wealthy, benevolent owner having his steward live on his grounds with him, to be ever at his disposal. As a reward for the steward's faithfulness, he would receive housing, food, clothing, pleasures, constant access to and fellowship with the owner.

- To sum it all up, the first picture ever of an owner/steward relationship is a picture of a life together, each trying to please the other. This is nothing short of the kingdom of God come to earth. Stewardship is not a despicable, but a privileged, position.

God is the owner; we are His stewards:

"Behold, the heaven and the heaven of heavens is the LORD'S thy God, the earth also, with all that therein is" (Deuteronomy 10:14).

"Know ye that the LORD he is God: it is he that hath made us, and not we ourselves; we are his people, and the sheep of his pasture" (Psalm 100:3).

"For we brought nothing into this world, and it is certain we can carry nothing out" (1 Timothy 6:7).

"Serve the LORD with gladness: come before his presence with singing" (Psalm 100:2).

All thievery begins when a man starts acting like an owner and stops acting like a steward. It is here where he separates himself from God. The first man became a thief when he lost his respect for God, neglecting his stewardship obligations, attempting to make himself equal with God, and reaching for food that was not his to have. Since then all men have stolen from God; all have eaten of forbidden fruit. All of us are thieves until we surrender to God. And let us take notice that man does not become a thief by stealing all that is in a store, but by just stealing one button.

Stealing and Our Stewardship to God

1. <u>As stewards, we cannot claim ownership or credit for anything</u>. We must give God all the glory for all things:

> *"For in him we live, and move, and have our being; ...For we are also his offspring"* (Acts 17:28).

> *"So likewise ye, when ye shall have done all those things which are commanded you, say, We are unprofitable* [worthless] *servants: we have done that which was our duty to do"* (Luke 17:10 [emphasis added]).

Therefore any accomplishment of man, whether in education, science, sports, industry or invention, is to be credited to God. Without Him, we cannot accomplish anything.

2. <u>As stewards, we must surrender our bodies to God</u>:

> *"What? know ye not that your body is the temple of the Holy Ghost which is in you, which ye have of God, and ye are not your own?"* (1 Corinthians 6:19).

Since our bodies belong to God, we must keep them undefiled. We must dress modestly, as becometh saints (1 Peter 3:3). We must not take our bodies where God will not go with us. We must not be gluttons.

3. <u>As stewards, we must give God all of our time</u>:

> *"Redeeming the time, because the days are evil. Wherefore be ye not unwise, but understanding what the will of the Lord is"* (Ephesians 5:16-17).

To "redeem time" means to rescue it from abuse. It means we use it to find and do the will of God. When someone asks us to do something that is not right, we tell them that we are living on God's time; we cannot and will not waste the time God has given us. In this modern era, we have to be especially careful with how we control media such as the Internet, Facebook and gaming devices in our daily lives. These take time away from God's plans.

4. <u>As stewards, we shall give an account of our deeds</u>:

> *"For we must all appear before the judgment seat of Christ; that every one may receive the things done in his body, according to that he hath done, whether it be good or bad"* (2 Corinthians 5:10).

"And I saw the dead, small and great, stand before God; and the books were opened: and another book was opened, which is the book of life: and the dead were judged out of those things which were written in the books, according to their works" (Revelation 20:12).

All of us are called to be God's workers; we have no other Master.

5. <u>As stewards, we will have to give an account over the use of the money</u> God has made us stewards over. This means we need to give tithes and offerings of our income. God calls people "robbers" who withhold their tithes and offerings (Malachi 3:8). In Matthew 23:23, Jesus reinforced the tithe. In Luke, Jesus enlarged upon it by saying:

"Give, and it shall be given unto you; good measure, pressed down, and shaken together, and running over, shall men give into your bosom. For with the same measure that ye mete withal it shall be measured to you again." (Luke 6:38).

All of our income shall be disbursed as the Lord Jesus, our owner, sees fit. If we treat our money as if it is our own, we are thieves.

Stealing is essentially taking God's label on what He has given us and replacing it with our label. Again, stealing begins with an attitude. Before man steals from man, he has already stolen from God.

Stealing and Our Stewardship to Man

Having noticed that stealing begins with God, we learn that stealing from man follows. As stealing from God is a violation of the First Commandment of love, stealing from man is a violation of the second law of love:

"Thou shalt love thy neighbour as thyself" (Matthew 22:39; Mark 12:31).

When we steal from God or from our neighbor, we must confess that sin, repent of it and make restoration for it. And God wants our restoration to be generous:

"If a man shall steal an ox, or a sheep, and kill it, or sell it; he shall restore five oxen for an ox, and four sheep for a sheep" (Exodus 22:1).

"And Zacchaeus stood, and said unto the Lord; Behold, Lord, the half of my goods I give to the poor; and if I have taken any thing from any man by false accusation, I restore him fourfold" (Luke 19:8).

Every sin against our brother is also a sin against God. Hence, when we sin, we not only

EIGHTH COMMANDMENT

erect a barrier between us and our brother, but also between us and God. Every time we steal, we harden our conscience until at last we are no longer able to discern that still small voice of God within us. Eventually, we begin to steal without our conscience convicting us anymore (1 Timothy 4:1-2).

Stealing from our fellow man has many faces. Many a college student has taken a pen from his roommate. Many a worker brings something home from the factory or the office. Then there is the house thief who slips a piece of jewelry into his pocket that he sees on the dresser of his neighbor. There is the church thief who steals from the church treasury. There is the business thief who extracts money from his clients by false weights and measures. There is the accounting thief who distorts the numbers in his bookkeeping. There is the lawyer or the insurance agent who withholds information or hides falsehoods in complicated legal language to deceive his clients. There is the landlord who exploits the widows and the orphans.

"Thou shalt not steal" also means that we should not extract labor from people without giving them their proper wages (Jeremiah 22:13).

However, stealing is not confined to money and property; it is also prohibited in relationship to our fellow man. For example, this command includes fathers and mothers depriving their children of the love, time, training and fellowship that are needed to make them strong. It also includes husbands depriving their wives of their time together.

"Thou shalt not steal" is first of all a call to the recognition that we are stewards and that God is the owner of all we have and of all there is. It means that we have no rights, but privileges to be the servants of the King of kings and the Lord of all, and that we should be content with that. Stealing from man always begins with us first stealing from God. Those who steal shall not inherit the kingdom of God (1 Corinthians 6:10).

Finally, there is this most heart-warming picture when it comes to the "End of the Age:" The owner will marry the steward and they will happily live together forever.

Questions to Ponder

1. Describe what all is involved in the birth of a thief? Begin with Eve.

2. In what sense have we all been thieves at one time or another?

3. What are the steps a thief must follow in order to get right with God and man?

Lying Corrupts Character

"He that speaketh truth sheweth forth righteousness: but a false witness deceit."

Proverbs 12:17

Ninth Commandment

"I am the LORD thy God...

Thou shalt not bear false witness against thy neighbour."
—Exodus 20:16

The previous commandments relate to attitude and actions. This one relates to speech: the prohibition of sinful speech. In the book of James of the New Testament, we read:

"For in many things we offend all. If any man offend not in word, the same is a perfect man, and able also to bridle the whole body" (James 3:2).

A man's speech reveals his character.

Jesus Simplifies the Ninth Commandment

Note that Jesus abbreviated this Ninth Commandment by leaving out the words, "against thy neighbor." <u>We have to remember that God the Father made His Son the final interpreter of the law</u>. In quoting this commandment, He simply said:

"Thou shalt not bear false witness" (Matthew 19:18).

The Apostle Paul did likewise (Romans 13:9). Here again, we find Jesus taking us further than anything that was written on the tablets of stone. Our Lord takes us beyond our immediate neighborhood to the neighborhood of all humankind. We owe each man and we owe God integrity of speech.

What Is at the Heart of this Commandment?

At the heart of this commandment is a call for truth: to think truth, to speak truth and to live truth. God will not accept anything other than truth. To Him, truth is not a matter of laws laid down by convention, nor a matter of majority vote influenced by cultural change and human progress. To God, truth is not a compendium birthed and nurtured in tradition. The Bible tells us that <u>God is truth and all truth flows out of Him</u>. God's truth is absolute. Therefore, truth is holy, truth is eternal, truth is immutable and truth is pure. Truth accepts no compromise, for God accepts

NINTH COMMANDMENT

no compromise. Advocates of truth cannot make her greater; adversaries of truth cannot make her smaller.

Truth cannot be meddled with. The whole cosmos came out of truth. Everything God did and does and will do bears witness to truth. All science came out of truth. If you have any untruth in mathematics, in chemistry, in physics, in biology or astronomy, these disciplines will become dysfunctional and useless. All of creation is saturated with the riches of God's truth. As a result, creation operates harmoniously, flawlessly and efficiently composing a great symphony of love, purity, power, majesty and glory. Jesus is full of grace and truth. Because Jesus is truth (John 14:6), and by Him all things are held together (Colossians 1:17), if there were any untruth in His creation, the universe would disintegrate. Anything that has untruth in it lacks cohesive power.

This has enormous implications for the Christian life. It tells us that the moment we speak a lie, we are out of harmony with God and nature. Our spiritual life begins to deteriorate at once. But if we speak the truth, think the truth and walk the truth, both God and nature will embrace us and commence to reveal their secrets to us. As children of truth, God will reveal to us *"...the treasures of darkness, and hidden riches of secret places..."* (Isaiah 45:3).

The renowned American scientist George Washington Carver committed himself to truth, and when he asked God what was in a peanut, God in time revealed to him 300 products that could be made out of a humble little peanut. God also revealed to him the coming of a mighty, worldwide revival.

The scriptures say that the Holy Spirit will guide us into all truth (John 16:13). Oh, what are the possibilities here? Can they be measured? If you abide in the truth and you are a carpenter, He will reveal carpentry to you. If you are a botanist in pursuit of truth, He will reveal botany to you. If you are an engineer, He will reveal to you the mechanical or electrical workings of things beyond what any man can learn from other men.

Oh, what all do we miss because we allow untruth to pull down the shades on truth? Paul said, *"A little leaven leaveneth the whole lump"* (Galatians 5:9). Untruth in the hearts of people, from the preacher to the banker, from the scientist to the politician, is one of the greatest impediments to the advancement of all that is right and noble for the good of mankind.

NINTH COMMANDMENT

Truth is light; untruth is darkness. All the sons of God are sons of light. Paul, the Apostle of Christ, said this:

"That ye may be blameless and harmless, the sons of God, without rebuke, in the midst of a crooked and perverse nation, among whom ye shine as lights in the world" (Philippians 2:15).

When Jesus spoke of the disciples as being lights of the world, He spoke of them as bearers of truth. So the Bible associates truth with light. John said:

"This then is the message which we have heard of him, and declare unto you, that God is light, and in him is no darkness at all" (1 John 1:5).

God is truth; any single untruth is an assault on all God is and all God does.

The Door of Salvation Is Shut by Untruth

Unless we come to grips with all deceitfulness in our lives, we cannot experience the new birth nor enter the city of God. But once we have dealt with all untruth in our lives, we are on our way. For Jesus said:

"But he that doeth truth cometh to the light..." (John 3:21).

Just one known lie in our lives prevents spiritual birth and growth. Lying is the work of the devil.

Jesus said to the Pharisees:

> *"Ye are of your father the devil, and the lusts of your father ye will do. He was a murderer from the beginning, and abode not in the truth, because there is no truth in him. When he speaketh a lie, he speaketh of his own: for he is a liar, and the father of it"* (John 8:44).

But Jesus came as the Light of the world saying:

> *"...I am the light of the world: he that followeth me shall not walk in darkness, but shall have the light of life"* (John 8:12).

Now, having been born of God, we need to walk as children of light (John 12:36). It is a daily assignment. Falsehood of any kind makes our light go out.

When Pilate, the Roman governor, said to Jesus, *"What is truth?"* (John 18:38), he took us to the greatest question of all philosophy. He took us to the beginning of a pursuit that, if we stay with it, will eventually lead us to freedom (John 8:32). There is no freedom outside of God.

The Devastating Consequences of Lying

1. <u>Lying is a sin and sin deceives</u> (Romans 7:11). If we are deceived, we take the truth to be a falsehood and falsehood to be truth. Because Eve

believed a lie, she was deceived. Everyone after her has likewise been deceived. Because of this, the people of Jericho mistook the best man in town, Zacchaeus, to be the worst. The Pharisees, having been deceived, took the Son of God to be the son of the devil.

2. <u>Everyone who holds a lie in his heart has a distorted picture of moral issues</u>. He cannot be trusted in his judgments: they will all be skewed, distorted. If we lie, our moral compass is off. It will lead us in the wrong direction and cause us to miss our destination. In other words, once we accept a lie in our lives, our spiritual seeing and hearing become impaired. We cease to perceive things as they really are. We become blind to the things of eternity (Ephesians 4:18). Because our first parents believed a lie, they lost their garments of light and found themselves to be naked. Everyone who harbors untruth is spiritually naked.

3. <u>If we lie, we cannot hear the voice of Jesus</u>. And if we cannot hear the voice of Jesus, we cannot follow Him (John 10:27). And if we cannot follow Him, we cannot be His disciples (Luke 9:23).

4. <u>If we lie, our life, our marriage and our business are on shifting sands</u>. Sooner or later, rains will descend, floods will come, winds will beat upon us; and what we have built will fall, for it was

not founded upon the rock of truth (Matthew 7:25).

5. <u>Whenever we lie, love flies out the window</u>. Love and lying cannot inhabit the same heart. If we harbor or cover a lie, we will not be able to love God, nor our neighbor, nor our spouse, nor our children, nor our parents, nor our enemies with the divine love of God. All our relationships with God and man will be broken, hindered, strained and stained. If we lie, we cannot be sanctified and filled with the Holy Spirit. We can only be sanctified through the truth. Jesus prayed:

"Sanctify them through thy truth..." (John 17:17).

6. <u>If we lie, our prayers will not be heard</u>:

"Who shall ascend into the hill of the LORD? or who shall stand in his holy place? He that hath clean hands, and a pure heart; who hath not lifted up his soul unto vanity, nor sworn deceitfully" (Psalm 24:3-4).

7. <u>If we lie, we bring darkness into our church</u>. Most churches are dark because too many of her members have hidden lies in their hearts. We know that there is something wrong in our churches. Often, we think the cure is in changing programs, but the real need is in the confession of all falsehood in the lives of the worshippers:

"God is a Spirit: and they that worship him must worship him in spirit and in truth" (John 4:24).

Truth and worship go together. God only accepts worship in truth. Here are a few more devastating effects of lying:

- Lying shuts out what God wants to do in us and through us, disqualifying us from the work of the kingdom.
- Lying strips us of our spiritual armor.
- Lying destroys Christian fellowship.
- Lying destroys justice.
- Lying brings disorder.
- Lying profanes speech.
- Lying impoverishes us, corrupts character and in the end takes us into hell:

"But the fearful, and unbelieving, and the abominable, and murderers, and whoremongers, and sorcerers, and idolaters, and all <u>liars</u>, shall have their part in the lake which burneth with fire and brimstone: which is the second death" (Revelation 21:8 [emphasis added]).

"Thou shalt not bear false witness against thy neighbour" means we must guard our brother's reputation. It means we should not betray, slander or defame another. Rather, we should put the best possible construction on everything about him.

If we want the rivers of living water to flow through us, we must be careful not to exaggerate. When we exaggerate, we are not telling the truth and the Holy Spirit is grieved. <u>As you can never tell when a liar is telling the truth, you can never tell when an exaggerator tells the truth</u>.

Because exaggeration, kidding, jesting, joking and foolish talk contain untruth, they should not be found among the saints of God (Ephesians 5:4). If we do these things, we stop abiding in Christ. If we are men of truth, we have the joy of heaven. Therefore we no longer need kidding, jesting, joking and foolish talk to lighten us up. God is not amused by our jokes. God never said anything foolish. He never used idle words. Man's humor finds no welcome in heaven. When Jesus taught us to pray: *"...Thy will be done in earth, as it is in heaven"* (Matthew 6:10), He meant that our conversation on earth should be as holy as that of the saints in heaven:

"But let your communication be, Yea, yea; Nay, nay: for whatsoever is more than these cometh of evil" (Matthew 5:37).

Paul adds to this:

"Let your speech be alway with grace, seasoned with salt, that ye may know how ye ought to answer every man" (Colossians 4:6).

"And my speech and my preaching was not with enticing words of man's wisdom, but in demonstration of the Spirit and of power" (1 Corinthians 2:4).

Not All Truth Is for Telling

There are times for us to withhold the truth. Truth is sacred. Truth is more precious than the finest of pearls. Jesus said:

"Give not that which is holy unto the dogs, neither cast ye your pearls before swine, lest they trample them under their feet, and turn again and rend you" (Matthew 7:6).

He means that when you know that the truth will be abused or made light of, it is to be withheld. Handle truth carefully and wisely. Once Jesus asked the Pharisces if the baptism of John was of

God or of man. The Pharisees, not wanting to be put on the spot, said:

"...We cannot tell. And he said unto them, Neither tell I you by what authority I do these things" (Matthew 21:27).

Truth told at the wrong time, at the wrong place and in the wrong spirit will do more harm than good. There are professional and military secrets that are not to be told. There is confidential information a pastor has that is not to be told. There is truth that some people, and sometimes our children, are not yet ready to receive. Paul said we should be led by the Holy Spirit (Romans 8:14). We need the Holy Spirit to know what to say and when to say it. Jesus said:

"...be ye therefore wise as serpents, and harmless as doves" (Matthew 10:16).

Untruth destroys justice and every bond of love. It brings disorder and invites every work of darkness. Do not bear false witness toward anyone. Do not lie for God said:

"...he that telleth lies shall not tarry in my sight" (Psalm 101:7).

Questions to Ponder

1. Where do we find the origin of truth?

2. What is devastating about untruths?

3. What will happen to you if you become totally committed to truth?

Covetousness Is the Mother of All Sins

*"What shall we say then? Is the law sin?
God forbid. Nay, I had not known sin,
but by the law: for I had not known lust,
except the law had said, Thou shalt not covet."*

Romans 7:7

Tenth Commandment

"I am the LORD thy God...

Thou shalt not covet

thy neighbour's house, thou shalt not covet thy neighbour's wife, nor his manservant, nor his maidservant, nor his ox, nor his ass, nor any thing that is thy neighbour's."

—Exodus 20:17

Covetousness is desire. In this Tenth Commandment, God condemns the desire within us to seek anything that is not ours to have. This commandment begins with a prohibition not to covet that which belongs to our neighbor. Coveting always begins in the immediate neighborhood where we are born. But as we grow up, our neighborhood increases, and we soon find the poisonous branches of our covetous nature spreading into the family of all mankind. The Apostle Paul abbreviates this command by simply saying:

"...Thou shalt not covet..." (Romans 13:9).

The Origin of Covetousness

Satan, also called Lucifer, the highest angel of God at one time, was cast out of heaven because of covetousness. He wanted to be like God (Isaiah 14:12-14). And in his first encounter with man, Satan planted this desire to be as God into the spiritual bloodstream of our first parents. Since then, we are all born with a covetous nature. Since then, we are all eating of the forbidden fruit:

"For from the least of them even unto the greatest of them every one is given to covetousness; and from the prophet even unto the priest every one dealeth falsely" (Jeremiah 6:13).

"For from within, out of the heart of men, proceed evil thoughts, adulteries, fornications, murders, Thefts, covetousness..." (Mark 7:21-22).

"And he said unto them, Take heed, and beware of covetousness: for a man's life consisteth not in the abundance of the things which he possesseth" (Luke 12:15).

Covetousness Precedes Every Sin

Covetousness is a disposition or attitude. There are sins of the flesh and there are sins of the spirit. Covetousness is a sin of the spirit, therefore it is the mother of all sins. For example, covetousness (desire) precedes idolatry (First Commandment), adultery (Seventh Commandment) and stealing (Eighth Commandment). Look at the lists of sins in Romans 1:29-31 and Galatians 5:19-21 and notice that all of them, in one way or another, spring out of covetousness. Covetousness is most wicked and carries within it the seeds of corruption and death. (Some believe that pride is the mother of all sins. But millions of people do not have pride; they suffer from a lack of self-esteem. Therefore pride cannot be the mother of all sins).

The Apostle Paul did not know sin in his heart until he came to the Tenth Commandment. As a Jew, he could say:

"Concerning zeal, persecuting the church; touching the righteousness which is in the law, blameless" (Philippians 3:6).

But once the Holy Spirit confronted him with the Tenth Commandment, he saw sin all over his life:

"What shall we say then? Is the law sin? God forbid. Nay, I had not known sin, but by the

law: for I had not known lust, except the law had said, Thou shalt not covet" (Romans 7:7).

"Mortify therefore your members which are upon the earth; fornication, uncleanness, inordinate affection, evil concupiscence, and COVETOUSNESS, which is idolatry: For which things' sake the wrath of God cometh on the children of disobedience" (Colossians 3:5-6 [emphasis added]).

When we covet, we are idolatrous. We break the First Commandment and, with it, all the rest of them.

What Is the Power of Covetousness?

Covetousness drives the human will. It is the silent, hidden governor in every man's heart. In the long run, it always overrides reason and revelation. We want what we want, even though reason and God tell us otherwise. There is nothing, absolutely nothing, more powerful than covetousness.

Covetousness is no respecter of persons. It drives the mightiest king (as greed) as much as the poorest pauper (as envy). It recognizes no borders and it has no respect for "keep out" or stop signs.

It is evident that, from the very beginning of the Bible, covetousness is the great spoiler of all that is precious, noble and pure. It is never satisfied.

Covetousness easily blossoms into desire run rampant. Covetousness cannot be cured by getting that which is not yours to have. When you deal with covetousness, you deal with the root system that makes a man what he is.

As long as we have a covetous heart, we will never come to rest in the city of contentment; rather, we live in the city of deception and false hopes because the covetous spirit keeps us running from one thing to another to find happiness. We must be delivered from covetousness. It makes fellowship with God impossible. As long as we have covetousness, we live outside the garden of God. We are slaves to our passions; we cannot win battles; and our prayers will not be heard.

Oh, what all have we suffered and lost because we have coveted? What all have we wasted in time, energy and money because we have reached for that which is not ours to have? How great is the damage we have done to ourselves and to others because of it? Can it be measured?

The Cure for a Covetous Heart

The cure for a covetous heart is not a changed heart, but a new heart, a holy heart, a meek heart, a contrite heart, a believing heart, a godly heart, a tender heart, a heart set free from sin. The Prophet

Ezekiel proclaimed this cure for man's wicked, covetous heart with these words 700 years before Christ came into the world:

"And I will give them one heart, and I will put a new spirit within you; and I will take the stony heart out of their flesh, and will give them an heart of flesh: That they may walk in my statutes, and keep mine ordinances, and do them: and they shall be my people, and I will be their God" (Ezekiel 11:19-20).

Notice the language here is not about a transformation of a heart, but about the replacement of a heart.

We cannot get rid of our selfish desires, lust, greed, pride, jealousy, impatience, anger, love of the things of the world and the lust of the flesh until we get a new heart. Man is as incapable of becoming his own savior as a goat is incapable of turning itself into a sheep. He cannot deliver himself from this selfish, carnal nature.

The Apostle Paul, as religious as he was, as well as he knew the Scriptures, as much as he prayed, and as much as he observed the religious rituals of his day, could not deliver himself from this awful lust of the flesh. As much as he tried, he ended up crying out:

TENTH COMMANDMENT

"For the good that I would I do not: but the evil which I would not, that I do" (Romans 7:19).

"O wretched man that I am! who shall deliver me from the body of this death?" (Romans 7:24).

Only God can deliver us. Indeed, we can put on sheepskins, but we cannot take on the sheep nature. Through education we can come to a measure of civil and moral refinement, but deep within us, the fire of the self-nature will continue to rage unabated (1 John 2:16). The old nature will continue to refuse to give up its own way. It will refuse to abdicate its throne. We need more than the trimming of our branches; we need a new root system. This is why John the Baptist said concerning our Lord's coming:

"And now also the axe is laid unto the root of the trees: therefore every tree which bringeth not forth good fruit is hewn down, and cast into the fire" (Matthew 3:10).

Jesus enlarges on this by saying:

"For a good tree bringeth not forth corrupt fruit; neither doth a corrupt tree bring forth good fruit" (Luke 6:43).

Again, to start with, we need a new heart. That is why Jesus said:

"That which is born of the flesh is flesh; and that which is born of the Spirit is spirit. Marvel not that I said unto thee, Ye must be born again" (John 3:6-7).

Baptism cannot make a new man out of an old man; partaking of Holy Communion cannot do it; church membership cannot give us a new heart; good works will also fail us:

"...all our righteousnesses are as filthy rags..." (Isaiah 64:6).

We must be born again!

The Prerequisites for the New Birth

1. We must confess both our sins and our sinfulness:

"If we say that we have no sin, we deceive ourselves, and the truth is not in us. If we confess our sins, he is faithful and just to forgive us our sins, and to cleanse us from all unrighteousness" (1 John 1:8-9).

2. We must repent of our sins with a determination to leave them behind and never return to them forever:

"I tell you, Nay: but, except ye repent, ye shall all likewise perish" (Luke 13:5).

3. <u>We must invite Jesus into our hearts</u>. Jesus said:

"Behold, I stand at the door, and knock: if any man hear my voice, and open the door, I will come in to him, and will sup with him, and he with me" (Revelation 3:20).

4. <u>We must forgive those who have injured us</u>:

"For if ye forgive men their trespasses, your heavenly Father will also forgive you: But if ye forgive not men their trespasses, neither will your Father forgive your trespasses" (Matthew 6:14-15).

5. <u>We must learn to follow Jesus</u>. Conversion belongs to one moment; following Jesus is our life calling. After conversion, the first step towards being followers of Jesus is self-denial. Right after the rebirth, we discover that there is something within us that does not want to witness, to pray, to give up wasteful television programs, attachments to the world and its toys, old ungodly friendships and habits. After conversion we find out that we still have a critical, murmuring, judgmental and self-seeking spirit.

This "something" within us comes under a number of different names, but they all mean the same thing: the self, the carnal nature, the Adamic nature and the old man. Within seconds after conversion, we discover that the self does not want to go along with us on this new journey with our Lord. It will protest, resent and resist any step we make in following our Master. Suddenly, we find ourselves in a war of the flesh against the spirit. That means, as soon after we have been born of God, we need to deny, crucify and keep crucifying the self and the carnal nature in order for us to follow Jesus. This is why Jesus said:

"...If any man will come after me, let him deny himself, and take up his cross daily, and follow me" (Luke 9:23).

As we deny self and obey Jesus, we are free to follow Him. We will actually begin to learn to walk with God, to hear His voice and to commune with Him as a friend communes with a friend. As we follow Him, we will be made into His likeness and be filled with the Holy Spirit.

Without self-denial and obedience, we cannot be filled with the Holy Spirit. We do not get the Holy Spirit at an altar. It is obedience that will invite Him into our heart (Acts 5:32). When that occurs, we find that we have come to the biggest thing in the world - sweet as honey, rich as cream, good as gold, fine as silver, refreshing as a stream; never tiring, never disappointing, always better than anyone had ever dreamed; it is beyond the

TENTH COMMANDMENT

orators of men to describe, colors to paint and the languages of earth to express; it is the kingdom of God on earth.

Do not covet. Again, to covet is to seek after something that is not ours to have. It will always bring us to disappointment, darkness and death:

"But godliness with contentment is great gain" (1 Timothy 6:6).

Questions to Ponder

1) What do we lose by breaking this commandment?

2) How can we be delivered from the covetous nature?

3) Consider how a violation of "each" of these Ten Commandments would affect your life, and the life of your family, church and nation?

Conclusion

What Is the Place of the Ten Commandments in Our Lives Today?

For the answer to this question we can go to contemporary theologians, we can go to church councils or we can go to the Apostles of old. But we shall do none of these. This question is of such weight that it bids us seek out the Authority of all authorities on it: Jesus the Christ! Here is what He said:

17 "Think not that I am come to destroy the law, or the prophets: I am not come to destroy, but to fulfil.

18 For verily I say unto you, Till heaven and earth pass, one jot or one tittle [a small mark similar to an accent] *shall in no wise pass from the law, till all be fulfilled.*

19 Whosoever therefore shall break one of these least commandments, and shall teach men so, he shall be called the least in the kingdom of heaven: but whosoever shall do and teach them, the same shall be called great in the kingdom of heaven.

20 For I say unto you, That except your righteousness shall exceed the righteousness of the scribes and Pharisees, ye shall in no case enter into the kingdom of heaven" (Matthew 5:17-20 [emphasis added]).

Notice these vital points from this passage:

- These commandments are binding on us, all the way through the church age until the end of time, because they have life in them.
- Breaking any of these commandments will continue to grieve the Holy Spirit. Lawlessness is against all that God is for.
- Whoever will teach these commandments will be highly honored.
- Our righteousness must exceed that of the scribes and Pharisees (who fasted, prayed, witnessed and were zealous for God) or we will be cut off from God (Luke 13:7-9; John 15:2).

The Law Will Affect Different People in Different Ways.

Both Jesus and the Apostle Paul put all people into three categories: the natural man, the carnal man and the spiritual man. In chapters 2 and 3 of 1 Corinthians, Paul makes these distinctions clear.

1. The Natural Man

"...the natural man receiveth not the things of the Spirit of God" (1 Corinthians 2:14).

The natural man is the unconverted man and to him, spiritual things are foolish. Therefore, **the natural man is indifferent to the laws of God.** He only interacts with laws insofar as they promote his own interests.

2. <u>The Carnal Man</u>

"For ye are yet carnal: for whereas there is among you envying, and strife, and divisions, are ye not carnal, and walk as men?" (1 Corinthians 3:3).

The carnal man is born again; he has come to Jesus, but is refusing to follow Him. That means he lives in the flesh and he therefore cannot satisfy the law's demands. Therefore, **the carnal man is frustrated by the laws of God.** In Romans 7, Paul describes the frustration the carnal man has with the law. Romans 8 describes the freedom from condemnation that the spiritual man has through abiding in Christ. By abiding in Christ, he fulfills the law.

3. <u>The Spiritual Man</u>

"But he that is spiritual judges all things... But we have the mind of Christ" (1 Corinthians 2:15-16).

Having the mind of Christ makes the spiritual man want what Christ wants, walk as Christ

CONCLUSION

walks, love and despise what Christ does. In short, he is one with Christ. Therefore, **the spiritual man delights in the laws of God** as his Lord's words. The law is not condemning him, but supporting him in his walk with God.

Jesus also discusses the three types of men. He called some cold, some lukewarm and some hot (Revelations 3:15-16). The cold are the unconverted and the lukewarm are the carnal. The carnal men had been hot, but they have lost their first love and are now lukewarm. Jesus despises them. The hot are those filled with the Holy Spirit.

Let us thank God for the law. It convicts, it converts, it illuminates, it fortifies us, it gives us inspiration and security. It blesses us. The spiritual man is not under the law, rather he stands on its strong foundations of righteousness.

Finally, the law is the metronome of the soul. By it, we know whether we are in step with our Beloved. Whosoever shall do and teach it shall be great in the kingdom of heaven. That is what Jesus said and what John confirms in these irrefutable words with which I shall close this book:

> *"And he that keepeth his commandments dwelleth in him, and he in him..."* (1 John 3:24).

Additional Resources by Reimar Schultze

ABIDING IN CHRIST: A 366-day devotional presenting helps for Christians to come to an intimate fellowship with Jesus (also available on Amazon as an E-book).

I AM LOVE: From Nothing to All Things: Pastor Schultze's autobiography shares the hardships of WWII, his search for God amongst its ruins, and his journey toward God's acceptable and perfect will with treasures abounding.

The Call to Obedience, a monthly letter (epistle), gives instruction and inspiration to help believers walk with God. This letter is available in several languages free of charge through Pastor Schultze's website: www.schultze.org

The Call to Obedience Radio, a weekly 15-minute radio broadcast, is available on the same website.

To order copies of Pastor Schultze's books, contact us at:

CTO Books
PO Box 825
Kokomo, Indiana 46903
www.ctobooks.com
E-mail: ctobooks@gmail.com